# POEMS OF L♥VE, LAUGHTER AND LOSS
# plus TRUE STORIES OF LIFE WITH GREYHOUNDS

## by

## JUDY ZATONSKI

## Foreword by
## JILLY COOPER CBE

# ABOUT THE AUTHOR

Judy Zatonski is 77 years old and lives in Rugby, England with her husband Mark. She has owned greyhounds for the past 28 years and currently has 5 dogs. These are two greyhounds Zosie and Kiki, two galgos Bambi and Freya and a lurcher called Lucas. They are all rescues.
Besides writing poetry Judy makes greetings cards and any money from selling her cards goes towards helping needy dogs.

# FOREWORD

## By Jilly Cooper

Judy Zatonski reminds me of Jean Anouilh's heroine Antigone, who felt she could never be happy if there were a single stray dog in the world. These are beautiful poems. Judy writes straight from the heart and in her case, it is a hugely loving, compassionate heart. Her poems will move you to tears but provide immense comfort if you are mourning the loss of a beloved dog or live in dread of losing one.

Judy's great love is greyhounds, she writes of them with such tenderness and poignancy, particularly the many who are cruelly treated or trapped in loveless homes.

What finally shines through is that our love for our dear dog friends is everlasting and we will meet them again once we cross the Rainbow Bridge.

Thank you dearest Judy

*Jilly Cooper*

*June 2016*

# CONTENTS

# CONTENTS                                          PAGE

# CONTENTS     PAGE

# CONTENTS

# POEMS
## of
## LOVE

# KIDS

On weekend mornings how we'd love
To have a lie in bed
But our two kids think differently
They want to play instead

At six o'clock or thereabouts
From sleep we both are woken
No longer can they rest themselves
And so our peace is broken

On the bed they leap with glee
And make a lot of noise
They bounce about both quarrelling
And fighting over toys

They won't stop pestering and so
Beneath the sheets we hide
They want our bed and not their own
And try to sneak inside

Our 'kids' comprise one boy, one girl
Their ages two and three
We're sure you know how boisterous
Kids of that age can be

We try ignoring their demands
And send them back to bed
But they're both young and neither heeds
A single thing that's said

At last we know we must give in
We're up and quickly dressed
The 'kids' have got their way again
The 'kids?' – our dogs – you've guessed

# EMMA

Emma, Emma, eyes so bright - what secrets do they hold?
A life so sad, a happy end - like a fairytale of old.


Once upon a time you raced; your heart and soul you gave
But tho' you ran you were not free, you were your master's slave.
How fast you flew around that track and oh how sweet success!
But all too soon the picture changed, you triumphed less and less.
Your owner had no time for you; your form it seemed you'd lost
No longer were you worth the price that racing greyhounds cost.
At five years old – no age at all – just like a worn out shoe
He cast aside that once prized dog, no further use were you


Your flesh stretched taut upon your frame, from sunken eyes you stared
What cruel world could do this thing, it seemed that no-one cared.
Then Sarah came into your life and nursed you every day
She restored your strength and confidence that had all but ebbed away.
Many, many months it took - with lots of TLC
'Til you were fit to be rehomed by a greyhound charity
Just like a fairytale princess of whom the stories tell
You triumphed over evil and broke the wicked spell.


Your brindle coat of black and tan is like a tiger's skin
Tho' marked just like a jungle beast – you're a 'pussycat' within.
You have the sweetest nature, such beauty and such grace
A cheeky sense of humour, that's pictured in your face.
You pose for lots of photographs, like supermodels do!
"Shall I lie this way or that?" – "Is this my best side too?"
Now you've Kevin and you've Rosy, to keep you company
At last you can experience how life should really be!

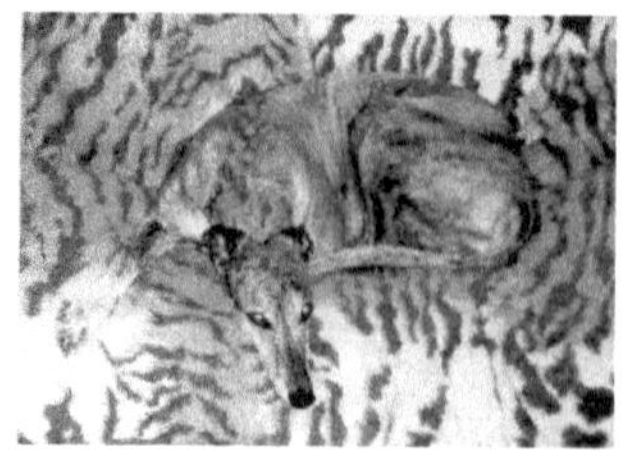

# AGONY & ECSTASY
(Dedicated to greyhounds racing in Spain)

A solitary dog stands on the beach
Reflecting - as the waves wash on the shore
The seagulls' cries are borne upon the breeze
As she recalls the life she had before.
Without a care and energy anew
The sand between her toes - she races free
A jeering crowd once shouted out her name
When Agony preceded Ecstasy.
For in the dusty, searing heat of Spain
And pads red raw from running on the track
Day in day out she tried to earn her keep
Till ev'ry ounce of strength she had was sapped.
Upon the concrete floor each night she lay
No comfort for her tired and aching frame
No-one cared - or tended to her needs
Each day that dawned would bring more of the same.
And when they broke her spirit and her will
And she had nothing left that she could give
Cast aside just like a worn out shoe....
None cared that she should die or she should live.
Each day she scoured the streets in search of food
Slowly growing weaker every day
Seeking warmth she curled up when night fell
And in a frozen huddle there she lay.
But God was looking down upon this hound
She heard him whisper "Do not give up yet"
A 'saviour' came upon this hapless girl
And snatched her from the jaws of certain death.
And so she came to stand upon this beach
Staring out across the tranquil sea
Her hopes and dreams at last were realised
And fantasy became reality

# MERROW

I raced as Wilcox Sunrise - 'Debs' - was my kennel name
When I retired and found a home – then Merrow I became.
Why Merrow? do I hear you ask - read on I'll tell you more
A 'Merrow's a kind mermaid …. from Irish Fairy Lore.
For I'm a stunning fawn colleen - from the Emerald Isle you see?
Westmead Merlin was my sire and a brindle dog was he
Hannah's a Rascal was my dam – I was born in ninety-nine
And though my racing I enjoyed – retirement suits me fine!!
On a website I appeared and Judy noticed me
(Her dearest Saffron passed away - a few months previously)
My 'home' was 'checked' (via mutual friends) – it seemed that all was well
For what the home might well be like – you just can never tell!
Now Mark and Judy only saw - my photo – on the 'web'
They never met me, all they knew, was that my name was Debs
So Els and Maurice drove me off – to Peterborough track
In August, on a Tuesday night and I've never since looked back.
The paperwork completed and my ownership transferred
Mark and Judy cuddled me - with reassuring words.
Part of their canine family – I have now become
And I get lots and lots of fuss - from Judy my new 'Mum'
Now Saffron was a 'model'... for a pretty girl was she
But I am on a calendar – 'Miss January' – that's me!
I don't like posing - but suppose...........a rabbit I should spot
'Mum' needs her camera ready and she'll get a cracking shot!!
Now when I hear 'Mum' get my lead – ready for a walk
I get excited, bark a lot and prance just like a horse!

I can't be called a greedy girl – like Inca (Jerry too!)
I eat my meals and clean my bowl – then go out for a poo!
I'm very fond of tripe sticks – and I like the odd pig's ear
We all get trampled underfoot - when the treat tin Jerry hears!!

* * * * *

When Saffron left it broke 'Mum's' heart - but it's truly my belief
That giving me a happy home - helped overcome her grief.
I have a really super life – I've been here four months now….
I've no more space – so 'Goodbye' all – it's time to take a bow.

# BESS

(Dear Bess passed away in 2005)

If you are sitting comfortably – then I'll begin my tale
I'm a pretty little black colleen – from the Emerald Isle I hail.
Let me introduce myself I'm Bess - yes that's my name
But I'm not like 'Bessie Bunter' - of literary fame
'Cos she was quite a buxom girl and I am very slight
(I needn't watch my waist and hips as many others might!)
I'm also known as Ballintee Pet - 'cos I used to race it's true
Us greyhounds have 'official' names – and we have 'pet' names too!
As I have said, back in my youth – I really loved to race
How fast I flew around that track and enjoyed the thrill of the chase.
Now time passed by and I slowed down but still I tried my best
When I was bumped and hurt my leg – they thought that I should rest.
My leg was bad, the healing slow, my injury may return
Because I could no longer race – my keep I could not earn.
My racing days now at an end... a home was found for me
This wasn't quite the happy place that it was meant to be!
I thought the people loved their Bess – it seems it wasn't so
Without my knowledge they had planned – this little girl should go...
And so they put me in the car – and drove away from home
They dropped me off and set me loose – and left me all alone.
Thirsty, hungry, tired and cold, I wandered aimlessly
(There surely must be someone - who would love and care for me?)
For days and days I walked the streets – I'd sores and lost my fur.
One day..............a lady pulled up in a van and took me off with her...
We ended up at kennels – oh! how damp and cold were they
And I didn't understand the words – "She's only seven days"
I didn't look a pretty sight – my future seemed quite bleak
With just a single day to go – before I'd 'done' my week.....
Someone said "Shall we try 'SAD' – (That's Auntie Shirley's place)
And when Auntie Shirley saw me – the tears streamed down her face
And so 'twas in the nick of time that Shirley rescued me
She sorted out a foster home where I lived happily.

With daily baths and lots of meals, with love and tender care
This pretty greyhound blossomed – four years I had been there…
When my foster Mum was taken ill – no longer could I stay
And so it was the second time that Shirley 'saved the day'
She found a lovely home for me – with Chris in Worcestershire
Her dogs have made me welcome and I'm really happy here
I live with Sophie, Tony too – with him I have such fun
We 'see off' garden 'visitors' – gosh – you should see them run!
I'm still quite slim but healthy now – I couldn't want for more
In bed I wear a nightshirt – but I'm not a girl to snore!
My Mum is always raising funds - for those less fortunate
So lots of people visit us – we dogs think it's just great
'Cos we get lots of human treats – 'their' biscuits taste so nice
"Bess - would you like this piece of cake?" - I don't need asking twice!
That I was born in '92 – did I forget to say?
But now that I've run out of space – I must be on my way!

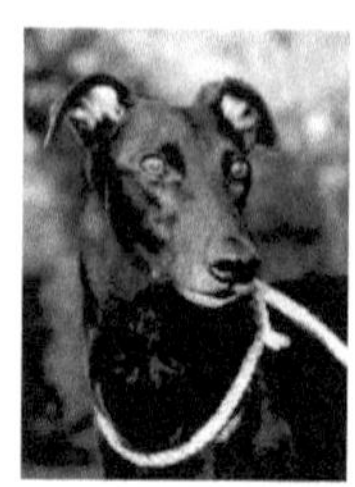

# THE HOUNDS IN BLACK

We're the boys and girls in black
A loving home is what we lack
People always pass us by
Although we try to catch their eye
We're left behind to wait in vain
Underneath we're just the same
We need your love, affection too
Why choose brindle, fawn or blue?
We're 'black beauties' all of us
Come and meet us – make a fuss
You'll see how loving we can be
We each are saying 'Please choose me'
Why does our colour matter so?
What matters is beneath you know
Our coats are black, our hearts are gold
Some are young and some are old
We've lots of love we'd like to share
Choose one of us and show you care
Please consider choosing 'black'
We promise that you won't look back

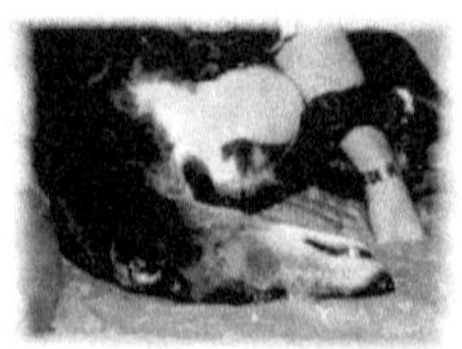

# THE PERFECT DOG

They came to find the perfect dog to join their family
Altho' they had a massive choice the one they picked was me

BUT……

I didn't match the sofa, I wee'd upon the floor
They said I took up too much space and that I scratched the door

They claimed I was aggressive that I didn't heed my name
It seems I was their 'whipping boy' for everyone to blame

I "didn't meet requirements" was the phrase they used
So I was taken back again frightened and confused

A day was all it took them to turn this hound away
How could this boy have learned the ropes in just one single day?

And so once more I waited as the visitors passed by
I felt somewhat despondent  as I tried to catch their eye

Then someone stopped to stroke me, my ears and chin they
scratched
Could this be my lucky day? (*Their* sofa would I match??)

And on that day they chose me…. but I was quite concerned
My confidence was shaken, in case I was returned

BUT…

I didn't have to worry and very soon I found
That they loved me 'warts and all' I was their 'perfect hound'

 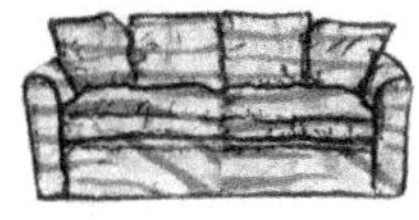

# GEORGE AND SALLY

This is the story of Sally and George
With Shirley they spent their days
They both now live at 'Rainbow Bridge'
For they have passed away
Their lives with Shirley were happy and fun
If you read on you'll see
So it's over to George to tell you his tale
If you're sitting quite comfortably!

Now as I have told you - my name is George
A grand Irish lad to be sure!
I first came to live with Shirley - my 'Mum'
When I was approaching four.
A big black boy – quite handsome of course
And as I was terribly strong
I had to be muzzled right at the start
But that didn't last for too long!
For I was quite gentle - that soon became clear
And I had good manners too
I'd not hesitate, to step back from a door
Allowing my 'Mum' to go through.
Those days the 'girls' were Ginny and Katy
And I was a gentleman too
Back from the park and needing a drink
I'd say to them both "After you".
Now I used to race at a Manchester track
The name I recall was Belle Vue
And tho' I'd retired, I was 'Dog of The Year'
Now that was in '92!
My 'Mum' was so proud I wore a 'posh' coat
I paraded around the track
But the only thing my 'Mum' now regrets
She's no photos on which to look back.
I'd just like to tell you about my career
(of which I'm decidedly proud)
Sixteen races - of eighteen I won
I can still hear the roar of the crowd!

At Christmas my former owners brought treats
And gave 'Mum' a video tape
Each time it was played and I heard the bell
I'd leap up and be ready to race!
It's Sally's turn now, in two thousand and one
'Mum' brought this pretty girl home
From a Liverpool yard, unwanted, unloved
Many days she'd spent all on her own.....

As George has just said Sally's my name
I'm a pretty fawn Irish colleen
And I fell in love with that gorgeous 'George'
The handsomest 'boy' I had seen!
Now as soon as it's light, I must wake my 'Mum'
Whilst George is still snoring away
I can't understand how dogs can 'sleep in'
It's a terrible waste of a day!
A handful of biscuits soon occupies me
(whilst George continues to snore)
I tuck into my treats and when I have done
I'll leave lots of crumbs on the floor!
Now I love my walks and I like my toys
As always - there follows a 'but'...
More than these things – oh! how I love food …
Most especially ginger nuts!!!
It's true that George raced, and I may have too?
But they can't trace my history
But my claim to fame? - I'm a sponsor dog
For GRWE.
The thing I hate most – being left on my own
'Mum' knows how worried I get
Whenever she can, she stays with her 'girl'
'cos if not - I'm likely to fret.

Now I'll bid you 'Goodbye' and George says "Farewell"
We're proud to share the name ''Brown'
Our 'Mum' loves us lots and we love her too
"Thanks 'Mum'"' from two grateful greyhounds.

# DEVOTION

How dearly do I love you - master
Touch me and my heart beats faster
Call my name – I'm by your side
A friend in whom you can confide
Your sorrow I will gladly share
And any burden you must bear
My love for you is steadfast, true
There's nothing that I wouldn't do.
A friend on whom you can rely
A shoulder on which you can cry
I know life's path is often rough
I'll be your rock when things get tough
When trusted friends all let you down
Put your faith in me - your hound

Please let me share in your emotion
And show the meaning of devotion

# WILF
### (The true account of Wilf's Rescue)

Let me introduce myself – my name is Wilf – that's me
I'm a really handsome greyhound boy – from my photo you will see
'Rahui Road' was once my name – tho' it seems I never ran
'Duke's Lodge' is what my sire was called and 'Open Road' my dam.
Now I was once ill-treated – and was locked up in a shed
And if I'd not been rescued then – I could well now be dead
This may sound quite dramatic – but believe me – it is true
I hadn't been looked after and my leg was broken too
Maria's daughter saved this boy – she used a cunning plan
She found a uniform to fit and then she loaned a van
She called upon my owner and she banged the door quite hard
When he asked where she was from – she flashed her library card!!
"I've come to take your dog away – yes, that's why I've been sent"
And I was rescued on the spot – then to the vet I went.

My life these days is filled with joy – there's nothing that I lack
I've so much to look forward to – I won't be looking back!!

# DOPEY aka Lopez
### Dedicated to 'Dopey' 2/1/95 – 31/12/2005

In ninety-five this boy was born - from the Emerald Isle he came
A handsome strapping brindle lad – 'Maryville Trixi' was his name
But in Ireland he did not stay – for Europe - he was bound
His name was changed to Lopez and to Rome they sent this hound
A sand fly bit this boy one day whilst at the track in Rome
He developed Leishmanaisis (much later this was known)
But then the racing track went bust and no-one spared a thought
For all the greyhounds kennelled there – who gave their lives for sport.
The future that these racers faced - was nothing short of grim
Hungry, thirsty …left to die – but then along came *GIN!
GIN rescued those abandoned hounds and some to England came
Wolker, Lopez and Pirata – three of these were named
And Northants Rescue took them in – a second chance they had
Where Mandy loved and cared for them – her three 'Italian' lads
For Wolker and Pirata too – a home for each was found
Whilst Lopez waited patiently – would no-one want this hound?

But then to 'Tailends' Lopez went - to Devon – by the sea!
He'd found a home with Angela – and pals for company.
This boy was nothing like a dwarf - (of Snow White story fame)
But not the brightest spark was he – so 'Dopey' he became.
And here his life began anew – with sand dunes to explore….
And one day Dopey wandered off and ventured to the shore
He came across the surfing school – a super sport it looked
And had he had some cash with him – some lessons he'd have booked!
Hang gliding fascinated him – he asked if he could try
But Angela said firmly "No" – it's only pigs that fly!

*GIN – Greyhounds In Need

But happiness did not last long ... this poem will reveal
Lesions started to appear – these wounds just would not heal
And as he didn't feel too well - he had to see the vet
They checked him over thoroughly and ran a lot of tests
Then Dopey's limbs began to swell and drugs the vet prescribed
Whilst Angela hoped desperately, the swelling would subside
Some days were good and some were bad – she wished she could do more
And when she was in town one day – she paused outside a door ..
The shop sold herbs .....she ventured in - fingers crossed in hope
And told the girl of Dopey's plight - but she no English spoke
But someone who could help was there - to translate English words
And Angela then left the shop - with a bag of Chinese herbs
At first this treatment seemed to work (it cost a lot of money)
And to help his ulcers heal – she bought Manuka honey.
Some times were those of dark despair but there were other days
When Dopey bounced with happiness and seemed to want to play
Rolling over on his back... and acting like a fool
But sadly it was not to be – for life can be so cruel
Just when it seemed there may be hope – (his sores had almost healed)
The Leishmaniasis took hold and Dopey's fate was sealed.
His abdomen swelled painfully – the vet was called and so....
Angela knew in her heart - she must let Dopey go
With deep regret and sadness too – there was no choice to make
The time had come to say 'Goodbye' – for Rainbow Bridge awaits...
for all those souls whose time has come – and life on earth is past
A place of freedom, joy and youth – a sanctuary at last
Dear Dopey if you're listening – your presence brought great joy
At last you can be free from pain – Rest in Peace dear boy.

# MIMI

You meant everything to me
My love, my life, my world
Why did you have to leave so soon?
My shy and timid girl
A privilege it truly was
To share our lives ... we two
I feel that there will never be
Another hound like you

I'm broken-hearted for I thought
We still had many years
To build your confidence yet more
And overcome your fears
My world will never be the same
Now that you are gone
But in my heart of hearts
I know life must go on

Oh how I miss my special girl
But tho' we've had to part
Your presence will remain with me
Forever in my heart

# THE GALGO
## (Dedicated to Gloria)


Four months each year she coursed the hare, beneath the Spanish sun
Her hunting skills were much admired by all who saw her run
Her eyes were focussed on her prey, she chased that hare at speed
Outstripping all the other dogs - she turned with utmost ease.

With hunting over for the year - their purpose they've fulfilled
These Galgos are of no more use and many hounds are killed
Inhumanely these dogs die – too grim to contemplate
Thrown down wells or hung from trees – often seal their fate
Some, could be called 'the lucky ones' for they are left to roam
Just like nomads - these hound live - all without a home
On the streets they can be seen , they scavenge to survive
Stealing food from anywhere - just to stay alive
And when the season comes again for coursing hare once more
The gypsies seek these Galgos out, to hunt – just as before

And Gloria was one such hound - by means more foul than fair
They captured her to work for them - once more to chase the hare.
And as the seasons came and went and Gloria slowed down
They cast this ageing bitch aside - preferring younger hounds.
So she sought refuge where she could  - starving, cold and weak
Her freezing body craving warmth - she curled up in the street.
Then Laura came across this girl - believing she was dead
Whilst weeping o'er her lifeless frame - this Galgo raised her head

And now she stands amidst the dunes and gazes out to sea
Her memories will slowly fade - of a life - that used to be.

# DANA

I'm a pretty greyhound girl and Dana is my name
In twenty-eleven I was born – from the Emerald Isle I came
Burnpark Champ my sire was called and Ballymac Floss my dam
Both of them were jet black hounds – but fawn is what I am
Now over 30 times I ran - around the racing track
I'm now retired and must confess -  I've never once looked back
My records show I've had some pups – that's twenty two in all!
But where they went and how they fared – I really don't recall
I came to England later on and crossed the Irish sea
Then Hector's Rescue took me in and Hayley cared for me
My new Mum Judy - spotted me – on the website so.....
Mark drove to Shropshire, picked me up... some several months ago
Little did I know back then - to Rugby I was bound
where I was welcomed 'doggy style' - by six excited hounds.
Silky, Darcy and there's Sprocket - (from the Durham pound)
Plus Warrick, Purdy, Freya too - they're Spanish hunting hounds
We dogs all get on very well – there's sofas by the score
And - a warm conservatory - what dog could want for more?
We're very lazy dogs you know? Of that there is no doubt
So when Mum wants a comfy seat – it's her that misses out
We occupy each vacant space – (We don't mind if we share)
But we're thoughtful... and at times – we'll leave our Mum a chair!!
Enthusiastic - yes that's me – when my walks are due
"Move over all you other dogs – 'cos I'm first in the queue!!"
That 'pigs might fly' the saying goes – it's true if you live here!
Watch out... a pink and fluffy pig – may just whizz past your ear!

'Cos I've discovered squeaky toys - much to Mum's dismay!
'Destroyer Dana' yes that's me – watch out – greyhound at play!
Beds are wrecked, the blankets ripped, my fervour knows no bounds
As I relive my puppy hood – denied of many hounds
I can't be called a greedy girl - tho' my meals I always eat
But I have a funny habit when my Mum gives me a treat
I don't stand there and eat it - like my 'piggy' galgo brother
I go and eat it on my own – then come back... for another!
My Mum takes lots of photographs – to capture my good looks
And 'cos I'm quite co-operative – I'm in my Mum's good books
But this may change as time goes by – as 'modelling's' a chore
I face the left and then the right – but still Mum asks for more!
But I may grace a calendar – 'Miss March ..or June' maybe?
Mum's had success in previous years... so there's still hope for me!
There's not much more for me to say – so I'll bid you all farewell
This is Dana signing off – one happy greyhound girl!!

# FERN

My mistress , Jo, wanted a greyhound
an ex-racer's what she had in mind
Good looking and sleek, blue-brindle maybe?
I'm sure you're aware of the kind.
So how did we come to be partners
me and my mistress Jo
I'm Fern and I am a lurcher;
well that **is** half a greyhound you know.
Am I sleek and blue-brindle in colour?
Not exactly – I've got to admit
'Only slightly hairy' is how I'm described,
tho' I'm sure that I have **some** sleek bits
From Sunderland pound I was rescued.
(Three times I was nearly put down)
At the 11<sup>th</sup> hour Margaret Gardener stepped in
– and that's when my life changed around.

Jo came with her husband to see me
Michael's his name – (so Jo said)
Maybe I flirted – well that's what girls do!
It seemed that I quite knocked him dead!!!
If you've got a minute to listen then,
I'll tell you 'bout some of my habits
I can jump really high, and like most of my breed,
I've a bit of a 'thing' about rabbits!
I was hot on the heels of a bunny
The barbed wire I just did not see
I was stopped in my tracks, my life hung by a thread,
Lady Luck must have smiled down on me.
When I'm resting I look quite amusing
a paw hooked behind one of my ears
They think I'm asleep but I'm listening
it's amazing what 'sleeping' dogs hear!
Well that's more or less my life-story,
there's not a lot more I can say
'Cept I'm pretty successful at Dog Shows,
with judges it must be the way
I hypnotise them with my beauty
it didn't take too long to learn -
Not bad for a dog that was rescued from death
a 'slightly hairy' lurcher named Fern!

# I ONLY CAME FOR BISCUITS......

I only came for biscuits
At the Pet Food Superstore
A bag of mixer and some cans
Maybe three or four ?
The shopping list gave details
Of all that I should buy
My neighbour asked if I would mind
As I was passing by
Some people were collecting...
Rattling their tins
I checked my purse for pennies
And put some small change in
They had some greyhounds with them
And fancy coats they wore
I quickly paused to stroke one
And he gave me a paw
I went to do the shopping
And came out laden down
With bags of this and tins of that
For my neighbour's hound
And as I hurried past them
A nose quite cold and wet
Touched my hand so gently
His sad brown eyes - mine met
"That's Billy and he needs a home"
I heard a lady say
"He's been returned to kennels 'cos
His owner passed away"
That second I was smitten
How could I turn him down?
I only came in for biscuits
And went home with a hound!

A home check would be required by most rescues

I'm her 'Spice Girl' my 'Mum' says - for Saffron is my name
I'm fawn and pretty (so I'm told) – from the Emerald Isle I came
I used to race – I'm now retired and home life is just great
I raced till I was over six – and now I've just turned eight
I have some funny little ways – 'Mum' often laughs at me
And when you hear the things I do – I'm sure that you'll agree!
I'm very fond of digging holes  (just copying my 'Dad')
He seems to think his holes are 'good' but my attempts are 'bad'!
Make certain that you close the door – if the loo you need...
(It's a piece of good advice - I recommend you heed)
For should I quickly flick my tail – just as I'm passing by
I'll whisk away the toilet roll – in the blinking of an eye!
I'll leave you high but far from dry - unravelling the sheets
Rewinding them is such a chore - to make the roll look neat.
My 'Mum' takes lots of photographs (I have such stunning looks)
But 'cos I find it tedious - I'm not in her good books!
She likes it when I prick my ears and look in her direction
She begs me to co-operate – whilst striving for perfection
But no amount of waving hands, or coaxing "Saffy – please!"
Or making noises like a cat – will make this girl say "Cheese"
Now sometimes when I'm fast asleep – my tongue falls out my
mouth
And then I look like 'Scary Spice' - of that there is no doubt.
When my 'Dad' goes off to work – we're early birds to rise
Each day he starts at six o'clock – we're walked before it's five

Like many other greys I know – I'm quite a lazy hound
And if my feet are not wiped first – I really must lie down!
Now if my meal is overdue and it's not served on time
I really feel I must protest by making sure I whine!
Because my jaw is overshot – my front teeth don't quite meet
I snap for fear of dropping it when 'Mum' holds out a treat
Although I could go on....and on... I'd hate to bore you so...
This is Saffy signing off – it's time for me to go!

...fond of digging holes

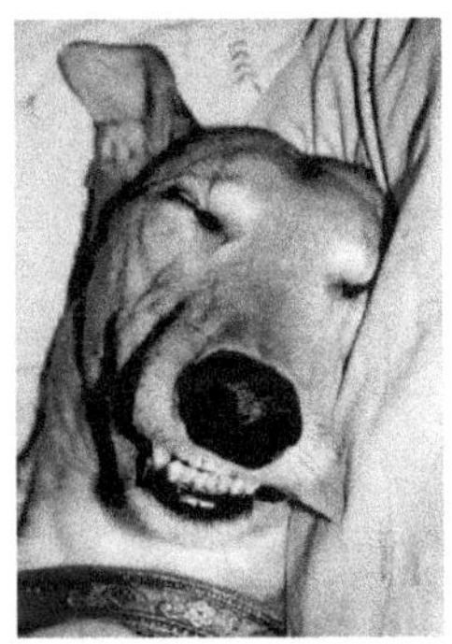

...my tongue falls out my mouth

# PLEASE

Please Oh please don't take me back
I've tried hard to be good
I'm not a disobedient lad
I'm just misunderstood

Please Oh please don't take me back
To the life I knew before
I really couldn't help myself
When I weed upon the floor

Please Oh please don't take me back
A chance is all I ask
But certain things I'm asked to do
Remind me of my past

Please Oh please don't take me back
This life is new to me
I'll do my best, I'll try so hard
Have patience and you'll see...

Please Oh please don't take me back
I'll try to 'learn the ropes'
But years in kennels locked away
Almost dashed my hopes

Please Oh please don't take me back
You'll surely break my heart
For years I've craved a loving home
And for a brand new start

You'll let me stay – not take me back?
Now I'm one grateful hound
You'll not regret it wait and see
For my love knows no bounds

# THE SUPERSTORE
(dedicated to Piper who was rescued from the same situation)

Tied up in the car park
Outside the Superstore
Abandoned by my owner
Not wanted any more

In the chill of winter
My lead was just a rope
Hungry – I stood shivering
I waited there in hope

Laden trollies passed me
Please give me a chance
The shoppers were too busy
To even spare a glance...

At this skinny greyhound
So cruelly cast aside
The day that I stopped winning
And hurt my owner's pride

The store would soon be closing
The shoppers heading home
Please show me compassion
Don't leave me here alone

With darkness fast approaching
I watched each person pass
Then someone stopped beside me
And there was hope at last

They stroked my head and whispered
You'll be safe with me
My rope untied – I followed
What fate awaited me?

# POEMS of LAUGHTER

# A FELINE ENCOUNTER

Poor Diane had a nasty fall
And grazed her knees and hands and all
Her jacket saved the other bits
Or she would have some scraped, sore tits!
Her trouser knees she'll have to patch
The squares she uses may not match!
Whilst walking her three strapping boys
A morning's stroll they all enjoyed
But when her concentration lapsed
Her lads espied a ginger cat
They all surged forward on their leads.
Di's "Steady Boys" – they did not heed
Temptation overcame all three
Next moment Di was on her knees
It shook her up – it would do me!
('Least no-one else was there to see)
To own a cat should be a crime
They wind the dogs up every time
They swagger with a bolshi air
Temptation's just too much to bear
To greys and lurchers they're great sport
Those pesky felines must be caught!

I doubt your lads know what they've done
They really have a super Mum
So Brendan, Boris, Billy too
Must see they take good care of you

# YOU DON'T MIND!

You don't mind my bobble hat
My woolly gloves - my scruffy mac
And I'm certain - you don't care
I haven't combed or styled my hair
I've faded jeans - unpolished shoes
These things - I'm sure don't bother you
You'll not notice my odd socks
Or that I dress from Oxfam shops
You're not fussed come rain or shine
Morning, noon or anytime
If the weather's cold or hot
I'm sure that you don't give a jot
It seems that nothing bothers you
But I'm aware this isn't true.......
For if you're overdue a walk
You'd say you'd mind -  if you could talk

# THE SNOOD

I have got myself a snood
It could be called a 'snuggle hood'
So Greys and Galgos listen hear
If you should want warm necks and ears
Get yourself a fleecy 'hood'
I guarantee they're really good
Your ears will be as warm as toast
But here's the bit you'll like the most
You can't hear your owner say
"Stop what you're doing right away"
You'll have warm ears, a cosy neck...
Plus an excuse for playing deaf!!

# MAC

I'm a really stunning greyhound boy – from my photo you will see
I have a tale I'd like to tell – are you sitting comfortably?
So if you're ready I'll begin  - What's my name? – it's Mac
And since I've found a loving home – I've never once looked back!
My name was different when I raced – and I was called 'Marks Joy'
And I was bred in the Emerald Isle – I'm a handsome Irish boy!
I have a proper pedigree – 'Rockmount Hazel' was my dam
My sire won the Irish Derby and he was called 'Eyeman'
My coat is rich red brindle and twelve months ago I raced
Retirement has now beckoned - as I couldn't stand the pace!
Greyhound Rescue, took me in (in Selby so I'm told)
And on the second of July - I'll be just 5 years old.
I live with Sarah, Richard too – I'm quite a lazy lad
But I can be quite naughty too – tho' I'm never really bad!
My duvet's in the kitchen and I love to take a nap
And just like lots of other 'greys' – I sleep upon my back
You'll often see this handsome lad – his legs up in the air
When 'Mum' and 'Dad' have gone to bed – I sleep in Richard's chair!
'Mum's good at putting food away 'cos I've been known to steal
She thinks that I'm not watching but I'm keeping my eyes peeled.
I once espied some muffins; choc chip - and made by 'Dad'
The smell was irresistible – too tempting for this lad
He left them on the unit – I just had to make them mine
And though my 'Dad' baked twelve in all – soon, I had taken nine!
I didn't take them all at once – just one by one I stole
The paper cases wouldn't shift – and so I ate them whole!!
I thought they wouldn't realise – the petty thief was me
But my bed was full of muffin crumbs for all the world to see!
'Mum's' parents live in Scotland and we go for holidays
They've dogs called Holly, Rosie too -  and on the beach we play

Now cats provide amusement 'cos to chase them is such fun
But squirrels don't play fair at all for up the trees they run
'Mum' says I am a 'monster' - 'cos I bark excitedly
I can see them in the branches – they delight in teasing me.
Now from my photo you will see – I'm wearing boots and so –
" Why is he wearing boots?" – folk ask...I bet *you'd* like to know?
Well I have corns, such painful things! (if you've suffered – you'll agree)
And so that stones can't hurt my pads - I wear these boots you see?
Although I've had to lose a toe –  I really couldn't care
I now enjoy my walks again – since I've had these boots to wear!
And now it's time to say "Goodbye" – my story is complete
I have a super life these days and I've fallen on my feet!

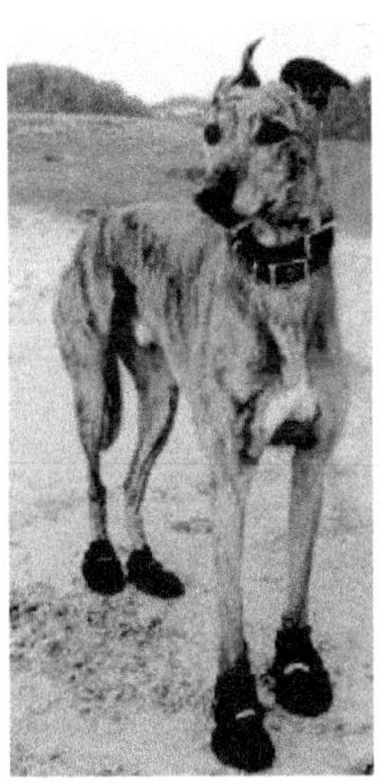

# WHAT'S IN A NAME?

What to call him – Rex or Sam
Charlie, Johnny, Bill or Dan?
Maybe Shadow 'cos he's black
Connor, Winston, Will or Jack ?
The choice is difficult to make
Piper, Shanty, Oscar, Jake?
Monty, Adam and there's Kerry
Lester, Jordan, Prince and Jerry
Duke and Tommy, Giles  and Jester
Noah, Matthew, Tom and Chester
Murphy, Austin, Harry, James
Why are there so many names?
Cracker, Taggart, Bond  as well
Trigger, Boycie, Rodney, Del
Max  and Bruno, Jarvis, too
Toby, Eric, Brendan, Blue
Phoenix, Bradley also Kenny
Ralph and Boris, Flynn and Lenny.
Archie, Monty, Todd and Luke
It's hard to find a name to suit
Norman, Henry, Bob  and Ricky
Snoopy, Freddie, Theo, Micky
Arnold, Leo, George  and Jasper
Sonny, Merlin, Bruce and Caspar
Scott or Wesley – even Joe?
Which to choose – we just don't know

You can tell we've racked our brains
Poring over lots of names ….
But WISIWYG's the best name yet
For **W**hat **Y**ou **S**ee **I**s **W**hat **Y**ou **G**et!

# PANICKY PARENTS!!!

Gosh! How our 'babies' worry us
It's no surprise we make a fuss.
Does Ben's leg hurt or does it  ache ?
(Stop fussing Mum – for goodness sake!)
Was that Brendan I heard cough?
Ben's on the bed – can he get off?
Does Billy have a runny nose?
Keep rubbing cream in Barbie's toes
(Poor girl – she has such pink sore feet)
Has Boris had enough to eat?
Is Brendan's 'poo' the solid stuff?
Does Boris' neck make him feel rough?
Does Ben's arthritis cause him pain?
He'll have to see the vet again
Can he make it up the stairs?
(Does Brendan have to wreck the chairs?)
The dogs are given pills  and potions....
Then we're asked to check their motions!
One tablet - three times daily - take
Will they rattle when they shake?
Drops for ears and drops for eyes
Primrose oil for balding thighs
Jabs for 'this' and 'that' disease
Yet more drops to ward off fleas
We poke and prod them all about
And hope that if it hurts - they'll 'shout'
We're vigilant for scrapes and bumps
And any strange and fatty lumps
Brush their teeth for breath that's sweet
And check they've no thorns in their feet
From head to tail our hounds we check
But still get huge bills from the vet!
Do other 'doggie' owners fret
At the slightest sniffle from their pet
I'm sure that many other 'Mums'
Listen out for rumbling tums
So – we panic – what the heck
Why fuss? Just write another cheque!!!!!

# ALL ABOUT 'ARRI'

Let me introduce myself – I'm Arri – yes that's me
And I'd like to tell you 'bout myself if you're sitting comfortably.
My name's not Harry (less the aitch) – it's short for Arrigle Go
I'm white and brindle, handsome too from the Emerald Isle you know
My sire was Arrigle Buddy and - what a 'busy boy' was he
Four-thirty offspring he produced – half-brothers and sisters to me!
I used to run at Wisbech track – I retired at three and a half years
One racing night – a 'rival' dog – bit off half my ear!!
And though this makes me look quite cute …… it was my 'Mum's' idea
to take the 'Mickey' out of me and call me 'Arfur Near'
Race Over Rescue in Kings Lynn - soon became my home
Then 'Mum' and 'Dad' came looking for – a hound to call their own
Now Flapper was another dog - who also caught their eye
I'm a macho and outgoing boy - whilst he was rather shy.
I raced around and wagged my tail - I'd impress them just you see!
And it was Arri's lucky day – for the dog they picked was me.
My life has been tremendous fun since the day they chose this lad
And tho' I have some naughty ways – I'm never really bad
The things I do, will no doubt put – a smile upon your lips
I'm very prone to stealing food but it never makes me sick!
First night - I spilled a jug of milk but I licked the floor quite dry
They do say over milk that's spilled – you really shouldn't cry!
Next day – some butter 'came my way' and I 'found' a loaf of bread
'Mum' would have made a sandwich - if I'd only asked – she said
A few days passed, when a Tesco bag, with doughnuts in - I spied
In less time than it takes to blink – they were lining my insides
But I overlooked the shredded bag and this revealed my crime
The sugar round my mouth as well – I'll take more care next time!!!
The story of the Bakewell tarts – I feel deserves a mention
To leave this box for me 'Dad' claims - was never his intention
He made a cup of coffee then – he looked round for his cake
The tarts were left at 'Arri' height - weren't they meant for me to take?

I 'came across' a box of eggs – I ate the yolks and whites
But the crunchy bits they call the shell – they weren't very nice!
There is one thing of which I'm proud – my most daring escapade
Mum lit the grill and four pork chops - beneath the heat were laid.
Temptation'd never been so great – what juicy chops were those!!!!
My quick reactions – they ensured  – I didn't burn my nose.
Now Mum was heard to say my breath – would 'fell a buffalo'
I had toothache - the vet proclaimed – "Four teeth will have to go!"
I confess that thunder scares me – (that's just ruined my street cred)
I cower underneath my quilt and quiver in my bed
But then my 'Mum' will sit with me - till the noises disappear.
And like a lot of other dogs – fireworks too – I fear!
And now I'm running out of space - though there's still more to tell
This is Arri signing off – I must bid you all "Farewell!"

# TERRY'S SIDNEY'S CHOCOLATE ORANGE *

Hi my name is Sidney and I have a tale to tell
I live with Jan and Penny too and Sexy Rex as well
Now generally – I'm well behaved but not quite all the time
I do have tiny lapses – when I lead a life of crime!
I hear I have an ally too – and Phoebe is her name
She's really fond of chocolate and I feel just the same
At Christmas for herself Jan bought, a very special treat
Without Terry's chocolate orange, Christmas wouldn't be complete
As Jan had eaten half of it – it's not like it was whole….
My conscience didn't prick me when this chocolate sphere I stole
Then hearing Jan's feet on the stairs – I quickly slunk away
But I left the wrapper in full view exactly where it lay
Jan couldn't be quite certain - which dog that it might be
But I think she had suspicions that the petty thief was me.
Now chocolate's irresistible – it has a super smell
If any treats are close at hand – be sure my nose can tell!
So when Jan bought another, to replace the one I took
And left it hidden in her bag – I had to have a look
But it didn't stop at looking – I had to steal this 'prize'
Now Jan could not believe I'd steal…..before her very eyes!
She stood there with an open mouth and stared in disbelief
For now it was quite clear to her that Sidney was the thief.
So I must learn that when I steal - a tempting chocolate treat
I must be stealthy, quiet too and most of all - discreet!

•Please be aware of the dangers of giving a dog chocolate

# TAKING THE BISCUIT!

A naughty dog, that was me – Saturday
I pinched some biscuits and then ran away.
For Caspar and Annie these biscuits were bought
Not once did I think that I'd ever be caught.
I devoured every morsel – the biscuits were great
Covered in chocolate – and all four I ate.
I couldn't resist that chocolatey taste
I made certain not one single crumb went to waste!
It's Monday today and I've stolen once more -
Some  'Cadburys' Shorties' were left on the floor!
Well that's nearly the truth – just a little white lie
In a carrier bag, this packet I spied.
The bag wasn't hidden – the biscuits they beckoned
Were they for me? Well that's what I reckoned!
Why leave temptation just lying around
Those biscuits were just crying out to be found.
Coated with chocolate and Cadbury's at that!
They were not made for sharing – but might make me fat!!
And so once again the whole packet was eaten
15 or more – I just wouldn't be beaten!
Tho' the wrapping was left as plain as could be
Folks couldn't be sure that the culprit was me
With four of us dogs – which one stole the pack?
Mark & Judy were cross but we didn't get smacked.
We did get a warning they made it quite plain
We just mustn't steal – not ever again!
But if I had the chance – I'd do it once more
They'd not know it's me (well they couldn't be sure!)
I'm a self-confessed 'Chocoaholic' no less
Which one of us four – I'll leave you to guess!

# A CRIME of PASSION

You heard about me and the biscuits
My lesson you'd think I'd have learned
Temptation's once more got the better of me
Surely one day my paws will be burned?
A present Mark had for his Birthday
Some 'Miniature Heroes' no less
You know I've a passion for chocolate
And Cadbury's sweets are the best!
Each day the huge tin was closed tightly
As the contents were gradually eaten
But I bided my time, one day they'd slip up,
My patience just wouldn't be beaten!
And then came the chance I'd awaited
The lid had been left off the tin
The choccies were left unattended
'Twas my chance to stick my nose in!
I had to be stealthy and quiet
And not make the others aware
For as with my other transgressions
I'm not very willing to share!
The wrappers made horrible rustlings
My collar disk clanged on the tin
I'd managed to scoff nearly all of the sweets
Before the three others joined in
I suppose I was really quite lucky
They treated us four dogs the same
And altho' it was me was the culprit
We all had to share in the blame
So – once more I've escaped being punished
I must have nine lives like a cat
Have I learned my lesson? Have you seen pigs fly?
I'm just a plain thief – and that's that!

** Please be aware of the dangers of giving chocolate to your dog **

# 'LET HER EAT CAKE!'

Would you believe it has happened again?
(It's a terrible habit of mine!)
I cannot stop stealing – but I'm getting more bold
It was under Mark's nose this last time!
He picked up his coffee and took a few sips
Before he tucked into his cake
I'd had my heart set on this chocolate treat
Since the instant that I saw the plate.
I bided my time till the moment was right
Mark's computer game held his attention
Then quick as a flash my teeth grabbed the cake
The words that Mark said – I daren't mention...!
I hurried away with my ill-gotten gains
To savour this treat at my leisure
Sometime it had been – since my last 'chocolate fix'
So my spoils would give me great pleasure.
Gosh! How my mouth watered as I slunk away
(I dribbled descending the stairs)
A shiny damp trail showed my getaway route
But at this stage I just didn't care!
As I lay in my bed, I savoured each bite
The first thing to go was the flake
Cadbury's chocolate I just can't resist
** For 'Exceedingly good cakes' they make!
The thing I regret - is that I was seen
It's a shame that my secret is out
No more will the others be blamed for my sins
I'm 'Phoebe the Thief' - there's no doubt!

** Mr Kipling make these for Cadbury!

** Please be aware of the dangers of giving chocolate to your dog **

# THE GIRL CAN'T HELP IT!

I hardly dare tell you what I did today...
Some luxury chocolates just 'happened' my way
And just as a criminal boasts of his crimes
I know it is naughty but I'm proud of mine.
A golden foil box – with a red ribbon tied
Held this chocolate selection safely inside -
Then having just savoured two, three or four
Mark and Judy resisted the urge to eat more
Scrumptious fillings with a rich creamy taste
Then back on the table the gold box was placed.
I watched and I waited – just biding my time
If I could be patient I could make those treats mine
I hardly acknowledged the chocolates were there
No sign of a dribble – no hypnotized stare
Completely disinterested – yes – that was me!
But looks are deceiving – as you will soon see.
You'd think I was sleeping, just resting my head
All the while I was planning the mission ahead
"Goodbye" to our visitor I heard them say
And they waved from the porch as her car drove away -
Now here was my chance - 'Opportunity Knocked'
And quick as a flash – I'd 'lifted' that box.
The chocolates were gorgeous – Belgian I think
They'd slipped down a treat – before you could blink!
I left the red ribbon with which they were tied
And a chewed golden box now quite empty inside
Then I heard Mark and Judy - on their way back
There just wasn't time to cover my tracks
The evidence lay on the floor in full view
I just couldn't help it – Honest! – it's true!

** Please be aware of the dangers of giving chocolate to your dog **

# I'VE MADE IT!

I've made it to the cover
of a greyhound magazine
So maybe I'll get noticed
when my picture has been seen?
It may not be a 'glossy'
'cos on them my sights are set
I maybe be eight - but as they say
there's life in the old dog yet!!
I must make sure my measurements
Are curvy... and yet trim
Sparkling eyes and nice white teeth
(Do I need to shave my chin?)
My walk is like a model's walk
Just watch how my hips sway!
I wear my 'Mum's' creations now
Top designer gear........one day!
Maybe........ I'll soon be noticed
Before it is too late?
I'd like to be a 'Cover Girl'
Like Naomi, Liz or Kate
If you're seeking out new talent
Then time you must not waste
I'm willing and available
Photographers – make haste!
I've made it to the cover
of a greyhound magazine
So maybe I'll get noticed
when my picture has been seen
Is this the gateway to success
To fortune and to fame?
Heads will turn and cameras flash
Remember......'Saffron' is the name!

## THE INVITATION

We three greys at home are waiting
Hoping for an invitation
Long ago we marked the date
When Wills would wed his darling Kate
We're Isla, Phoenix and Mimi
We've donned our wedding finery
We eagerly await the post
'Cos the thing we'd like the most
Is to join the chosen few
And proudly we would take a pew
So we three greys could give our blessing...
Just why is it? – they keep us guessing
Whether  we can go along....
And at the 'Abbey' join the throng
Unhappy faces you will see
If they overlook us three ....
Perhaps our invite's gone astray?
And we must put our hats away
How disappointed we shall be.....
We'll have to watch it on TV!!

# TEASING TULIP

I'm sitting here just thinking, as I watch the rabbits play
Why **is** it? – when they see me - that they run the other way?
I don't **really** want to hurt them
But the chase is such good fun
It's just the way that I've been trained
For I was born to run.
So I'm sitting here just thinking
As through the glass I stare
If they knew that I was watching
Would they still be playing there?
I'm sure they love to tease me
They know I'm shut inside
If I could have my freedom
They'd run away and hide
I'm sitting here just thinking,
As I watch the world go by
How I'd love to chase those bunnies
You'd see how I can fly!
It's really just a game to me
Oh I could have such fun
If they loosed me in the garden,
Then you'd see those bunnies run
But as I sit here thinking, watching from my sofa bed
Maybe I'll not give chase today but curl up here instead!

# HOW ARRI GOT HIS ASBO

Arri is a greyhound - Retired from racing now
But Arri's got an ASBO - Read on....he'll tell you how!!

Now one day it happened just purely by chance
I saw the front door wasn't shut
My Dad had forgotten to close it up tight
'Opportunity Knocked' for this mutt!
In the kitchen was Mum she was making the tea
and suddenly - I had a thought
Why drag her away – No - that would be mean
When I could just go for a walk!
Oh what fun it was – as I wandered along
For once I was out on my own.
No Mum and no Dad at the end of the lead
I needed no chaperone!
Unaware I was out and enjoying the sun
Was a cat in a garden close by
Maybe it stretched or it moved in some way?
Whatever it did - caught my eye!
The training I'd had all those years long ago
Flooded back... and so I gave chase
Boy – was I fast - and the cat was quite old
It just couldn't keep up the pace.
'Twas not my intention to end this cat's life
But I carried it home all the same
It wasn't my fault – it didn't run fast
Surely I wasn't to blame?
Mum and Dad were aghast at my 'feline faux-pas'
But I wasn't told off – it is true!
To see the cat's owner – both thought it wise
For that was the 'right thing to do'
Tho' the owner was sad at losing her pet
She said that she quite understood
But wishing like mad, I could turn back the clock
I knew wouldn't do any good.
Mum and Dad didn't know the police had been told
It naturally came as a shock
To find an officer dressed in plain clothes
At the door - when they answered a knock

What happened and when and why and how
Was I likely to do it again?
A new gate was planned – we had a high hedge
Her utmost Mum did to explain.
The hedge was too dense, to tall and too deep
For me to attempt an 'escape'
And without a long run (or a Fosbury Flop)
I'd never get over the gate!!!
Fingers crossed, that was it - the 'cat-case' was closed;
For that was what Mum and me thought!
'Til a letter arrived and Mum was dismayed
For she had been summoned to court.
'A Dangerous Dog' – the policeman had said
After he'd interviewed us
A dangerous greyhound? That's surely not me?
I couldn't believe all the fuss!
I've not many teeth just a few at the front
As 'Goofy' - is what I am known
'Dangerous' – moi? – I know I did wrong
But out of proportion 'twas blown!
So Mum went to court and in my defence
She explained just what had occurred
Dad left the door open – it wasn't my fault
She protested ...... nor was it hers!!
On deaf ears this fell and my 'sentence' read out
As poor Mum, the magistrate faced
An 'ASBO for Arri'  the court had decreed
A 'control-order' on me was placed.

Am I the only greyhound
With this 'claim to fame'
Ashamed or proud – I'm not too sure?
'ASBO ARRI' is the name!!!

** This is a true account of what happened to 'Arri

# 'A CAPSULE A DAY KEEPS THE VET AWAY'

My dogs take Evening Primrose Oil
Two capsules every day
They say it keeps them healthy and..
Their aches and pains at bay

Now three of my four canine pals
Take capsules willingly
Leah leaves an empty bowl
As do greyhounds - Brad and 'Fee'

But when I mix up Roscoe's meal
And hide his pill with care
When he's finished you will see
His tablet lying there!

Cod Liver oil my friend's dog takes
For a healthy coat that shows
Would it give *me* glossy locks?
(But not a cold wet nose!!)

Now Bradley suffered balding thighs
For hair to grow – we wished
Several things were thought to help
And one was oily fish

The sardines helped his hair grow back
And so my husband said
"If I eat sardines will the hair
Grow back on my bald head?"

But he was just a touch concerned
Would hair grow on his head
Or would it grow where Bradley's did
Upon his bum instead?

# POEMS of LOSS

 MUCH MORE

I love you more than words can say
More than a sunny Summer's day.
More than the moon that shines at night
Giving out its ghostly light.
More than the stars that shine on high
Twinkling in the evening sky.
More than the gentle Autumn breeze
Rustling through the coloured leaves.
Much more than birds that sweetly sing
And soar above on feathered wings.
More than a chilly Winter's morn
When trees with hoar frost are adorned.
Much more than Spring's refreshing showers
Bringing forth a thousand flowers.
And as the seasons come and go
I love you more than you will know,
My love is constant, steadfast, true
As every day I think of you.
Altho' this life you've left behind
You are forever on my mind
You're with me still - tho' we're apart
You are forever in my heart
Each day I love you more not less
So many thoughts – but none express
Just how much love I feel each day
Much more, my friend, than words can say.

# PARTING

There'll come a day when we must part
But our friendship will remain
I'll wait for you at Rainbow Bridge
And we'll meet up again
Until that time we must enjoy
Each moment, every day
The happy times, the sad times too
Whatever comes our way

And should you get another pal
To keep you company
Don't think I'll mind - for I will know
You're not disloyal to me
You'll stroke his head and call his name
How happy he will be
Your love for him will be as strong
As is your love for me
And as the months and years roll by
Dear Friends may come and go
And some may slumber in my bed
I will not mind - you know

There'll come a day – I don't know when
I'll leave this life behind
Parting will be oh so hard
But courage we must find
To say "Goodbye" - but we both know
Our love will never die
Our memories will never fade
Tho' many years pass by

So when I take my leave of you
I know there'll always be
A special place within your heart
That you will keep for me.

 # DON'T FRET

Don't fret dear friend, the time has come
For us to say "Goodbye"
I must be strong and hide my tears
So you don't see me cry.
I mustn't let you sense how much
This grief tears me apart
That I must ease your suffering
I know within my heart.
It's easy to be selfish and
think only of **my** sorrow
Clinging to the vainest hope
that you'll be here tomorrow....
But I must only think of you
and cast despair aside
You need me more than ever now
I see it in your eyes.
Oh why is it so hard for me?
To free you from your pain
My love for you is endless
for that is what I claim.
Don't fret dear friend – the time has come
For me to let you go ...
For you it is the kindest thing
Within my heart I know
I hope you will forgive me
As you  drift away my friend
Our life together here on earth
Is coming to an end
Please understand this thing I do
Is in the name of love
Thank you for your trust in me
And unconditional love.

# SO SOON FORGOTTEN

A TRIBUTE TO BOBBY aka Moral Director

With ev'ry sinew straining
And ev'ry muscle taut
With eyes completely focussed
To win each race he fought

Back then he was victorious
He always ran his best
And from the track he heard them
Shout his name above the rest

His owner loved a winner
And doted on this boy
He often heard him boasting
"Yes he's my pride and joy"

He fathered many offspring
A sire of wide acclaim
There wasn't any breeder
Who didn't know his name

But as the years rolled onwards
And young dogs took his place
Folks often asked with pity
"Did *he* ever win a race?"

The trophies now are dusty
They once held pride of place
No longer are they cherished
Just like the dog who raced

In a kennel now imprisoned
Where no-one cares a jot
Exists that once loved winner
Mankind so soon forgot.

# BEFORE YOU GO

Before you go I want to say
How much you mean to me
A friend more loving, loyal too
There will never be
Before you go please understand
Why I must do this deed
You put your faith and trust in me
In this, your hour of need
Before you go – please do not fret
Should others come to stay
Your mem'ry will remain with me
Forever and a day

It's time to go – be still - my friend
Slip away in peace
The angels will watch over you
Nor will their vigil cease

# WE'LL MEET AGAIN

When finally I breathe my last
And life upon this earth is past…
We'll miss each other oh so much!
Each will crave the other's touch.
But tho' we've had to say 'Goodbye'
Our memories will never die.
The happy times – the sad times too
The 'ups and downs' we've both been through
Farewell dear friend – but do not fret
For we shall be together yet
Your journey one day too, will end
We'll be united – two 'lost' friends
At 'The Bridge' we'll meet again
And life will once more be the same
Through years to come our love will last
Look to the future not the past

# IF LOVE COULD HAVE SAVED YOU

If love could have saved you
You'd never have left -
Left me alone....
And feeling bereft

If love could have saved you
You'd never have died
For you'd still be with me
Close by my side

If love could have saved you
We'd never have parted
You'd never have left me
Distraught, broken-hearted

If love could have saved you
You'd never have gone
Now only my memories
Still linger on

If love could have saved you
You'd still be here
And I wouldn't be living
Alone with my tears

If love could have saved you
You'd have not said 'Goodbye'
I constantly miss you
As each day goes by

If love could have saved you
You'd have lived on forever
So strong is my love
That we'd still be together

# HOW MANY TIMES?

How many times will I quiver in terror
as I wait for his hand on the door?
How many times must I suffer a beating
until I can't take anymore?
How many times will I tremble and cower
when he's reaching out for his stick?
How many times will I seek a safe haven
before he delivers a kick?
How many times will I cry out in pain
from a cigarette held to my chest
How many times am I frightened of sleeping
when my body is aching for rest
How many times will he claim I've been naughty
and chain me outside in the rain?
How many times must I shiver with coldness
whilst my body is wracked with pain?
How many times will my poor bones be broken
and my bruises and cuts need to heal?
How many times - I given up counting...
is this how other dogs feel?

But....too many times you dealt a kick
Too many times you raised your stick
And now my life on earth is past
And I will feel no pain at last
Your cruel hand has sealed my fate
But peace at Rainbow Bridge awaits

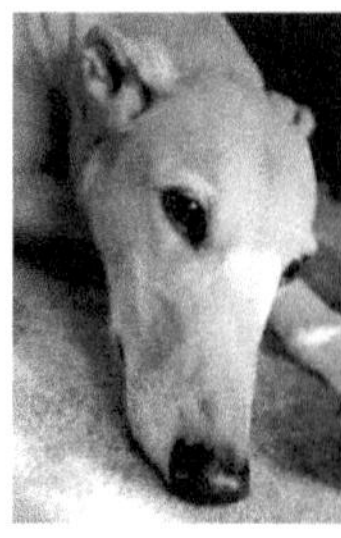

# HOPE FOR HARRY

(This poem was written for a competition run by the Dogs' Trust
and was highly commended)

It's not that Harry wasn't wanted, he was wanted very much
He didn't ask a lot of life - just his master's loving touch.
But for Harry – like his master, 'old age' was creeping fast
They could no longer be together - and the life they shared was past
The two companions said "Goodbye" -
Their eyes were moist with tears
The master – he had found a home
To spend his twilight years….
The rules were plain "No pets" they said
No dogs allowed to stay
And each one's heart was broken
Upon that fateful day
The two friends parted company
And Harry's life became
A lonely one in kennels
Like those who wait in vain….
For that special place called 'home' - a warm and cosy bed
For someone who'll return their love and see that they're well fed.
For who would want poor Harry now – his coat had lost its lustre
No longer could he play all day – he'd no energy to muster
Consider those who fell from grace - just because they're 'old'
Through no fault of their own it seems - they're turned out in the cold.
Those dogs who have a chequered past and those 'unruly' hounds
Those too - with disabilities….for them – will homes be found?
Like Harry – there are many - with stories of their own
Each waiting for that 'someone' who will offer them a home.

# THE ANGELS

The angels carried you away
When I was fast asleep
But in my dreams they promised me
A vigil they would keep

And on their silent feathered wings
They bore your soul away
You heard them softly call your name
As in sleep I lay

They promised they would care for you
With all the other hounds
At the place called Rainbow Bridge
Where freedom knows no bounds

And though we've gone our separate ways
Dear friend - please do not fret...
I know our paths will cross once more
We'll be together yet

# I WISH

I wish that I could turn back time
To that day we met
Your big brown eyes stared up at me
That look I'll not forget ....
They said "Please take me home with you
I'll be a loyal friend
No matter what the future holds
I'll love you to the end"
A younger dog I did not crave
I knew time would be short
For all the riches in the world
Your health could not be bought.
We cherished every single day
We knew it could not last
I hoped my love would help you to
forget about your past.
Oh how can life be so unfair?
Some time is all I asked
In my heart of hearts I knew
That you were failing fast
We had just weeks – not months or years
So precious was each day
I wanted you to know true joy
Before you passed away
I begged you 'Please don't give up yet
Don't leave me now my friend
Our life together's just begun
Please don't let it end'
But as I said these words I knew
The truth I'd have to face..
So take my love with you my friend
To a safe and peaceful place
I wish that I could turn back time....
I know this cannot be
If I was granted just one wish...
You'd still be here with me

# WIZARD

Such a dear black lurcher boy – at least you had a name
You were ED five-one-o – but Wizard you became
But you were very poorly - when you left the pound
Weak and very skinny - but we hoped you'd rally round
With a name like 'Wizard' we had hoped you'd have a spell
To help you to recover and to make you fit and well
But ….you couldn't eat or drink – as in your bed you lay
You couldn't even raise your head on that fateful day
And so we had to call the vet - to end your suffering
Oh Wizard – how upset we were – to have to do this thing
Such a dear black lurcher boy – at least you had a name
We loved you then – we love you still but now you're free from
pain

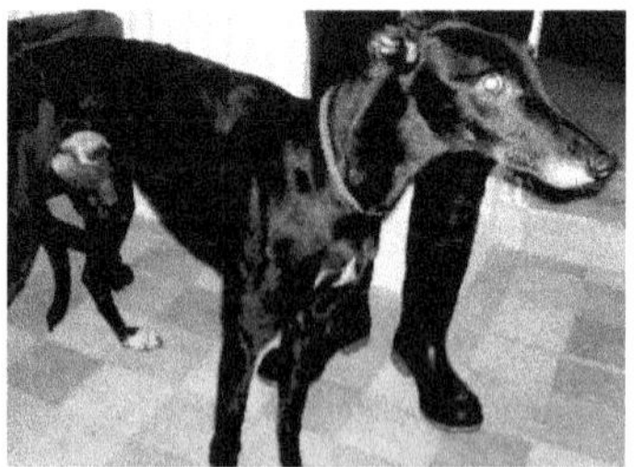

# COMFORT ME

Lay your hand upon my head
So I can feel your touch
My eyes are dim but let me see
That face I love so much
My limbs are weak - so lay with me
And hold me very close
You are my very dearest friend
The one I love the most
I cannot speak and so I put
My faith and trust in you
Because your love for me is strong
You know what you must do
Let me feel you by my side
I want to feel you near
Whisper words of love to me
Those words I need to hear
The time has come for me to go
The Rainbow Bridge awaits
And all those hounds who've gone before
Are waiting at the gates..............
To welcome me – so "Farewell" friend
I must be on my way
Hold me tightly in your  arms ..
But wipe your tears away
We won't forget the happy times...
we've shared – both you and I
It's time to go – but there's no doubt
Our love will never die

# THE CHAMPION

My owner had great plans for me
A champion ...one day ...I'd be
My sire was famous – and my dam
From good breeding stock I am
The 'perfect pup' I heard them say
He'll make us rich – for sure – one day
I realised my owner's dream
And triumphed on the racing scene
Winning races by the score
But greedy humans still want more
And as the months and years progressed
'Twas clear that I was past my best
So a stud dog I became
For all the breeders knew my name
I fathered offspring but alas
No great winners came to pass
It seems I'd hurt my owner's pride ...
'The Champion' was cast aside

An air-gun pellet sealed my fate
I lie here in the ditch and wait
For death to bear this boy away
The 'champion' of yesterday!

# A BETTER PLACE
### Dedicated to all the forgotten hounds


Please spare a thought for those poor hounds
who die devoid of love
Though no-one cares for them on earth
God watches from above
For when they're called to Rainbow Bridge
here - all the caged run free
The starved are fed and watered
like every dog should be
The beaten and ill-treated
will now be free from pain
The outcasts and the strays alike
will find a home again
So when their lives are over
to a better place they'll go
To join the happy carefree hounds
at Rainbow Bridge and so........
They may not be remembered
when on earth  their days are done
But God is watching over them
each and every one.

# NOW THAT YOU ARE GONE

I hope you heard me tell you
how beautiful you were
Such stunning looks, such big brown eyes,
such soft and shiny fur
I hope you heard me tell you
What joy you brought to me
You cheered me up when I was down
You were a friend indeed
I hope you heard me tell you
You kept me company
When others had 'too much to do'
To spend some time with me
I hope you heard me tell you that
You never let me down
Always there, my friend, my rock,
when others weren't around
I hope you heard me tell you
Just what you meant to me
A friend who never blamed or judged
Just 'there' as friends should be
I hope you heard me tell you
For all I've said is true
Wherever you may be dear friend
Please take these thoughts with you

# THE VIGIL

Altho' we've had to say goodbye
My vigil I will keep
Each night watching over you
As you soundly sleep
Your guardian angel I've become
I move without a sound
Each night watching over you
Your cherished, faithful hound
My days are spent at Rainbow Bridge
My spirit running free
But each night watching over you
Is where I want to be
Tho' you'll not see me when you wake
To visit you - I've been
Each night watching over you
Appearing in your dreams
And as you slumber peacefully
I softly call your name
Each night watching over you
United once again
And tho' no longer flesh and blood
For all eternity
my spirit lives... until once more
Together we shall be

# MY DEAR FRIEND
### In memory of Ben Campbell

Dear Friend ..... I had to let you go
'Twas harder than you'll ever know
Never one to make a fuss
You had to take your leave of us
I never once heard you complain
How bravely you endured your pain

You soldiered on – but now alas
Your life down here on earth is past
How gladly I'd have borne your pain
To see you fit and well again
How I wished it could be me
Alas Dear Friend – 'twas not to be

My tears I will not try to hide
I feel that you're still by my side
Your coat feels soft beneath my touch
I mourn your passing oh so much!
I know Dear Friend this had to be
In spirit - you are still with me

I know that I'll shed many tears
As I recall the past few years
Tears of sorrow – also joy
As I remember my Dear Boy
May God Bless You – tho' we're apart
You're here forever in my heart

All my love

# IN REMEMBRANCE

This tribute is a canine prayer
For gentle greyhounds everywhere
Those cast aside, the waifs, the strays
Who've not known love for all their days
Those abused, abandoned too
The beaten – still forever true
The cowed, the lost, unwanted hounds
Awaiting life, or death, in pounds
Our hearts go out to every one
From loved and true companions...
To those who crave an owner's touch
And need our love so very much.
And as we speak these heartfelt words
Please God just let our prayer be heard

# A SPECIAL PLACE

I feel that you are sleeping
altho' you'll never wake
Inside I feel so angry
that God your life should take
I know he must have called you
"Come now – it's time to go"
He must have had his reasons
but why I'll never know
And though you're sleeping soundly
you're always in my heart
Though you've been taken from me
we'll never be apart
And though I cannot touch you
when I close my eyes I see
Your trusting, loving, handsome face
looking up at me
And though the pain gets easier
it never goes away.....
It's comforting for me to know
you're with me everyday
I feel you're watching over me
in everything I do
Within my heart there'll always be
a special place for you.

# DON'T MOURN TOO LONG

(Inspired by a short verse by Joyce Grenfell)

When it's time for me to go
And we have said farewell
Please don't mourn for me too long
But try to sing as well
Sing about the happy times
And let the sad times go
Fill you heart with joyful thoughts
For life's too short you know?
Speak of me with fondness and....
Recall our special days
Hold dear those happy memories
That time cannot erase
Each wouldn't wish we'd never met
Tho' now we've had to part
So walk again the paths we trod
But not with heavy heart
Don't close the door upon my life
Just because I've gone
In your heart ...and in mine too
Our friendship will live on
Should you prepare a grave for me
To lay my soul to rest
A simple headstone with my name
Is what I'd like the best
Or if my ashes you'd prefer
To scatter far and wide
You'll watch the breeze bear me away...
Yet feel me by your side


Be happy that our lives we shared
On sadness do not dwell
Maybe shed a tear or two?
But will you sing as well?

# RAINBOW BRIDGE

The Rainbow Bridge awaits - my friend
The journey's not too far
A shaft of moonshine lights your path
To guide you there's a star
Your friends are there to welcome you
You'll meet old pals again
They're waiting at 'The Bridge' my friend
Calling out your name
Don't be afraid – you'll be quite safe
You cannot lose your way
For many souls have trod this path
As each is called away
Go join the hounds at Rainbow Bridge
Forever running free
And though this earth you've left behind
In spirit you're with me

# HOW FAR?

"How far is Rainbow Bridge?" - you ask
"Not very far" - I say
We both know that the time has come
For you to slip away...
"Will I lose my way?" you ask
"Oh No – of that I'm sure"
The path has been well trodden by
Those hounds who've gone before"
"Will *I* be safe?".... I hear you ask
"Don't be afraid" I say
"The angels will watch over you
And guide you on your way"
"Will I meet old pals?" you ask
"They're waiting just for you
And as you're welcomed at the gates
They'll see you safely through"
"Will we meet again?" you ask
"We shall – I'm sure" I say
"I'll come to join you at 'The Bridge'
When I am called away"
"Is it time to go?" you ask
"It's time - dear friend" I say
"Put your faith and trust in me
And gently slip away"
Let your worries melt away
There is no need to fear
For though you've left this earth behind
In spirit you're still here

'Have you reached 'The Bridge?' I ask
I'm here - both safe and sound
And though we two have had to part
Still by our love - we're bound

# LISTEN

Listen – can you hear your name?
He's calling you – my friend
Although you're slipping from me now –
This is not the end...............
A new life is about to start
Where you'll be free from pain
Old-age - you'll shrug off like a cloak
And you'll be young again
Listen – can you hear Him call?
His voice is soft and low
And as you leave this earth behind
Remember - as you go.......
I'll not forget you my dear friend
Though we may be apart
Your mem'ry will remain with me -
Forever, in my heart
Listen -  He is calling still
Reaching out and so.....
Take His hand and slip away
It's time for you to go
So many happy times we've shared
These, sadness can't erase
For we shall be together still
Tho' we've gone separate ways
I'm listening - but there's no sound
You must have heard His voice
We both knew that the time had come
We knew there was no choice
You've breathed your last – your eyes are closed
But this is not the end.......
For life at Rainbow Bridge awaits
Rest in Peace – dear friend

# WHEN I SAY FAREWELL

Will you stay close by my side – when I say farewell?
Will you softly stroke my head and comfort me as well?
Will you whisper words of love and will you say my name?
Will you reassure me that - one day we'll meet again?
Will you say for certain that there's nothing I should fear?
Will you still remember me - when I'm no longer here?
Will I meet old friends again – do they know to wait ….
Will you say I'm on my way – so they are at the gates?
Will you join us at the bridge....although you don't know when
Will we be together...will we one day - meet again?

# STORIES

With thanks to Andy Hammond for the illustration

# A STREET GIRL

Hi – I am Bambi a Galga (Spanish greyhound) from Spain. I was found on the streets at 18 months old – rescued and then I came to England just before my third birthday..

I was originally called Brandy but I am now Bambi due to my agility and I have acquired a couple of nicknames like most dogs do. One is Bam Bam (from the Flintstones cartoon I am told) and the other is Bambino – however, when this term is used it sounds more like Bambi 'NO'.

Apart from being an over-protective guard dog - I have only one other small fault (that I will admit to) and that is pulling on the lead. I do wear a gentle leader which helps curb my enthusiasm but where we dogs are walked there is a wealth of fascinating smells. At night various wild animals come out to forage for food and play – these include rabbits, badgers, hedgehogs and muntjac deer….so you can imagine how exciting it is for us dogs! Although the field where we are walked has mown paths, there are still large swathes of long grass harbouring the best smells. Whereas small dogs can't be seen in these areas – unfortunately we long-legged hounds are always visible so can't disappear into the wilderness. However, I view this groundwork as valuable research in case David Attenborough decides to produce a second series of 'Life in the Undergrowth' and wants me in a starring role!

Well - life here in England is a far cry from Spain and I think I am going to enjoy my future years if the past couple are anything to go by!!

# MONKEY BUSINESS

Some years ago Greyhound Rescue West of England held an auction in aid of the needy hounds. I donated a couple of items and decided to get out my needles and knit an 'ITV' monkey to add to the lots. This proved well worthwhile as 'he' was sold to the highest bidder for a massive £250!
A few years down the line – I thought that in between making cards, tassels and bandanas I would once again pick up my knitting needles and produce another monkey. I started on the 'easy' bits – the body, legs and arms as the face is quite a challenge to say the least.
Each time I finished my knitting session I carefully put my work in a carrier bag – well out of harm's way – or so I thought.
It would seem however,  that a young endearing greyhound called Inca, is exceedingly inquisitive and anything new must be investigated thoroughly...... doubtless to say this included my carrier bag.
One weekend, Mark and I thought we would pop into town for an hour or so – the dogs had been out in the garden to relieve themselves where necessary and as is customary, they were all given a tripe stick on our departure. Giving them one of these when we go out has an ulterior motive – we needn't suffer the rather pungent odour associated with these apparently irresistible treats!!

On our return it appeared that is wasn't just the tripe sticks that had grabbed their attention.
The carrier bag containing my knitting clearly appeared to have been the focus of 'someone's' curiosity.
Just as a person holds out their arms to accommodate a skein of wool ready to be rolled into balls – the legs of the dining room table had been put to similar use. Yards of grey wool were now trailed round and round the legs and obviously having finally tired of this undertaking, what remained of the original ball lay in a tangled heap on the floor.
Although Merrow has been known to run off with the odd ball of wool on this occasion I am pretty sure that the culprit was Inca!
She clearly had much more fun unravelling the wool than we did winding it up again. I suppose I was lucky that the knitting itself was still intact and she had not gone as far as removing the stitches from the needle.
So Mark found a new string to his bow and kindly assisted me in performing several circuits of the dining room table to retrieve the wool and then becoming 'chief untangler' whilst I wound the wool into a ball.
In future, the carrier bag will be placed high up – well out of reach of any inquisitive canines!

# THE SAFFY SHOE SHUFFLE

Well, I suppose it's really more of a 'skulk' than a 'shuffle' but whatever word you use – the long and short of it is that Saffy steals shoes!! Sandals, trainers, lace-ups, slippers – she's not fussy what type of footwear and if shoes are in short supply – then a sock or two will do instead. She doesn't really chew them to the point of being destructive but I think the word that's used for leather jackets and the like is 'distressed'. Just a few teeth marks give the game away - plus the fact that you can never find a complete pair. Just one slipper or a single trainer and then the hunt is on! I can never attempt to go out in a hurry if I have yet to locate my shoes. OK - one is where I left it but the other could be anywhere and my little 'tea-leaf' is unlikely to lead me to her ill-gotten gains. Oh well – I know full well that greyhounds are prone to petty pilfering so why should I think Saffron would be any different? She may have a 'butter-wouldn't-melt-in-my-mouth' expression but looks are so deceiving. She has such a happy demeanour you can't be cross with her for long and anyway in the meantime I can always wear another pair of shoes! My husband Mark doesn't call me Imelda Marcos for nothing!!!

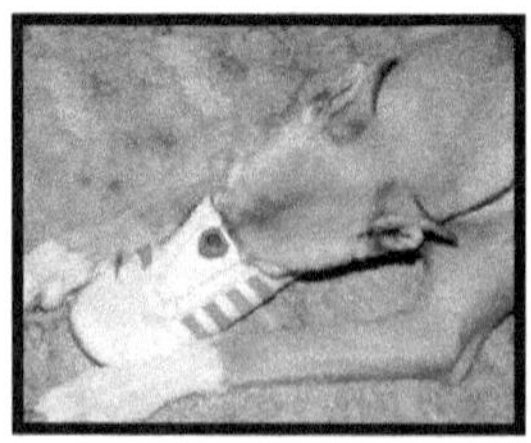

# JOY BRINGER

Yes – that's me a Bringer of Joy!
It's hard to tell the truth and be modest at the same time but my 'Mum' says I have really brought so much joy to her life. Although I was called True Lass when I was born in Ireland in 1997, my name was later changed to Joy – Jamstyle Joy that is, when I raced at Perry Barr track in Birmingham. I enjoyed my racing days for that is what I was trained to do and I suppose I must have brought Joy to all the people who backed me when I won my races.
Then at the beginning of 2004 I was retired aged six and a half and I spent my days in kennels, with a companion, waiting to see what the future held for me now that I was no longer fast enough to compete in races. I was pretty shy – well pretty and shy are probably better descriptions and I hid at the back of my kennel when visitors came to choose a dog to share their home with them. Never having experienced 'home' life, this was unknown territory and I wasn't sure whether this was how I wanted to spend my future.
However, when the time came (in April 2004) I didn't have a choice in the matter and I was taken out into the paddock so my prospective owners could meet me. They had lost their dear Phoebe to cancer just two days previously. Well – at first I stayed at a safe distance from them as I didn't want to appear too keen but they stroked me and said how pretty I was and within a couple of minutes they had decided that I should go home with them.
Despite my reservations, home life was nothing to be scared of after all and although I am still wary of strangers after nearly two years here – I can honestly say that home life is wonderful. I am called Saffron these days mainly because of my rich fawn colour. When I am with the folks I love – my shyness is a thing of the past and I am bouncy, affectionate and enthusiastic. I may have brought Joy to my Mum and Dad's lives but they have brought immense Joy to mine.

SAFFRON

...stayed at a safe distance

Joy Bringer!

# STOP THIEF!!

Although the title is very apt maybe it would be more accurate if it read "DOOR STOP THEIVES" The plural refers to both Inca and Merrow as they are both guilty of stealing – as are the majority of greyhounds I have come across. Inca's penchant is for the plastic wedges that are used to keep doors open and allow a through draught but at the same time prevent the doors from slamming shut. The sound of a door banging is therefore a sure sign that Inca has been on a pilfering spree. However, not only does she steal them – she also 'customises' them. I now have several wedges with a multitude of teeth marks and parts of them missing altogether – the 'thin end of the wedge' might be a fitting phrase except that it is the thin end that is missing. Fortunately when I realised this was not a passing fetish, but it was a habit that was here to stay, I managed to locate some metal wedges that (so far) appear to be 'Inca-proof'. Unfortunately, the shop only had two of these in their sale and so I had to be content with these. Then "Eureka" I spotted a square, stuffed fabric door-stop about the size of a house brick and equally as heavy, to hold back the door. It was in an attractive burgundy colour with a large, black material bow on the top. This was duly put into action in place of one of the vandalised plastic wedges.

My elation however, was short-lived. Merrow – who seldom plays with any of the multitude of toys at her disposal, has taken a liking to this door-stop. She can frequently be seen wandering off with it and giving it an occasional shake. Woe-betide any dog passing by, who is oblivious to the impact that this swinging door-stop could have if it made contact! The weight of this object appears to be of no consequence and seldom can the door stop be seen doing its job in preventing a door from slamming. Having resigned myself to this becoming a plaything for Merrow, I went to purchase another. When I asked if they still had stock, I was informed by the shop assistant that they had sold out of this particular style but they did have some in the shape of animals. I suppose it was foolish to expect one shaped like a dog to stay in situ for any length of time but I blithely bought one and used it in place of the 'stuffed square'. In a trice the 'dog' disappeared too – not unexpectedly I might add – but now not only Merrow steals these padded door stops but Inca does too, having changed her affection from the plastic type. Metal ones seem to be the only option left to curtail the antics of these door stop thieves.

# INCA

As many of you may know from experience, when you have a two-year-old in the house, you need eyes in the back of your head – well having a two-year-old greyhound is no different! Even in their dotage, greyhounds are dyed-in-the-wool thieves but a two year old is just that bit more nimble. Our previous greyhounds have all been 4 years or older so a two year old – or slightly less as she was then, was quite a shock to the system. Nothing could be safely left unattended – and most especially food. Greyhounds have exceptionally long noses and exceedingly long legs and can reach parts that others cannot. Work surfaces are like a coffee table to a 'grey' and I must admit it has taken me quite some time to adjust to coping with a very inquisitive youngster. My baguette disappeared whilst my back was momentarily turned and had it not been in a paper bag – which gave the game away – there was not a crumb to be seen. My doughnut went 'walkabout' whilst making a cup of coffee and I don't know how she did it – but there was not even a trace of sugar on her chin. I won't begin to list all of her other conquests – but suffice to say we are quick to react to 'unusual' noises. These are her only downfall and if she ever learns stealth tactics – God help us! Now Inca is a very endearing girl but house training her proved (and is still proving) quite a challenge. ....

We tried the 'clicker' method which is all very well but if the dog doesn't choose to relieve itself whilst out for a walk – then there is no point in 'clicking'. Once back indoors Inca proceeded to wee on the carpet – so it was back out into the garden. However, by this time she no longer needed to go.. Right – plan B – get a crate! They don't foul their own space – we were told - so she won't wee in a crate! Obviously the voice of experience had yet to experience an Inca! Wee in her crate – no problem - poo in her crate – she could do that too. Well we have eventually got her to perform during a walk or in the garden if necessary but she still manages to have the odd wee indoors – not on the floor which is easy to mop up – but on a dog bed or similar. (Each bed now has it's own internal waterproof cover – just IN CAse!). So when we go out – she is put in the cage. She goes in quite willingly (with the assistance of a tasty treat of course) and she can see the other dogs so she is not alone as such.  However, she still has a few 'accidents' in the crate – so we are a bit stumped on how to overcome this problem. Well she is only two…… will we still use a similar excuse when she is ten??

The other thing Inca does to amuse us, is that when she shakes her head whilst out for a walk, her tongue flops out of her mouth and there it stays! She walks along looking like the 'village idiot' – Sorry Inca but it's quite embarrassing walking along with you in this state!
We do love you really!!!

# GOLD DIGGER!

No – not a dog that digs for gold but a gold dog that
digs!! Yes it's that Saffy again. When we chose
Saffron our 'BFG' (Beautiful Fawn Girl) to fill the void
that our dear Phoebe (Kenmare Zip – ex Perry Barr)
left in April 2004, we were led to believe that she was
a quiet, shy retiring girl – that she may have been…
but she is certainly not now!!

Phoebe

I know comparisons are odious but these two girls
are so similar in nature – Saffy appears to have
stepped straight into Phoebe's shoes. (And talking of
shoes – both are guilty of stealing footwear!) Saffron
is more affectionate than Fee but both can be
described as stubborn and uncooperative and they
both seem to have an affinity for newly raked earth.
We had just removed a variety of overgrown herbs
from a rockery and raked over the soil ready for
replanting when my brindle girl took up residence.
You are no doubt familiar with the plants Phlox and
Hebe but this is a Phoebe of the genus Greyhoundius
Zatonskii.....

Now maybe Saffron feels the need to imitate
Phoebe's traits so that I don't miss my dear
departed girl too much – and she has surely
succeeded. This time we had removed some
wayward plants from a flower bed, planning to turf
over the area in due course - when Saffron decided
that we needed help. Having wiped his brow and
put the spade away, Saffron took up where her
'Dad' left off and put her digging skills into action.
Four pristine white socks very soon became four
brown ones and after her exertions – of course –
she needed a lie down! Saffy's help resulted in a
much larger hole than we had anticipated – so we
now just hope she is as good at filling in as she is
at removing the earth.

Saffy – you never
cease to amaze and
amuse us with your
funny ways.

# EARLY MORNING WAKE-UP CALL 

If you ever need to wake up early in the morning and you don't have an alarm clock – why not borrow Saffron? She is as reliable as an alarm clock and equally persistent until she can be 'switched off!' Three o'clock is about the usual time although occasionally it has been as late as 4am. This early morning call begins with a faint whine which gets progressively louder if I don't respond to her demands.
I encourage her up on the bed in case she is in need of a cuddle but No! this is not the reason she has woken me at this unearthly hour. So, knowing why dogs usually whine, I reluctantly get out of my nice warm bed and take her downstairs. I pad across the kitchen floor which is freezing to my un-slippered feet, locate the back door key and then stand there shivering with the door ajar, waiting for Saffy to go out into the garden to relieve herself. She peers out of the door, twitches her nose at the chilly air and stands there as if to say 'I hope you're not expecting me to go out there in the cold?' I must admit, you could never accuse her of having a weak bladder as she can go for hours without needing a wee!
What can the reason be that she has woken me at this early hour with her persistent whining?
Perhaps she's hungry?
And that was the answer – little minx! A handful of biscuits and she was happy to go back to bed and sleep for another three or four hours.

This occurrence however, was not a one-off!  Like clockwork,  practically every morning around 3 or 4 o'clock the whining commences. I have a couple of options…..firstly to turn over and do my utmost to ignore these simpering cries. In this case however, ignorance is not bliss and the whining does not abate if I attempt to ignore her. It just gets louder. My other choice is to go downstairs as before, just in case this time the plea is a more desperate request and Saffron really does need to go outside. A few mornings of braving the cold and standing at the back door with a totally uninterested greyhound peering out into the dark, has eventually convinced me that she isn't in need of a wee!

Food – that is the sole purpose for her demands. She can never be called a greedy dog as she is not generally motivated by food but it would seem that hunger pangs strike in the early hours of the morning – each morning to be precise – and Saffy must have sustenance!

The solution………. a tin of biscuits at the bedside, within arms reach, so that a couple of treats tossed in her direction put a stop to the whining and we can both go back to sleep without even leaving the comfort of our beds.

# CANINE ON THE CATWALK!

As you probably all know, besides writing PoETry, my 'Mum'
makes lots of things to raise money for the needy hounds.
The items she produces include greetings cards, notelets, dog
bed covers, tassels, bandanas and coats. However, in order to
show people what the majority of items look like, 'Mum'
always volunteers me to model them. Although this is tiring,
unpaid work with unsociable hours, I feel that it is my duty to
do my bit to raise money for the dogs that are far less
fortunate than me. At this point I must make it clear that
getting recognised by one of the top fashion magazines has
absolutely nothing to do with my co-operation whatsoever!
However, I do know that some of Phoebe's pictures appeared
in Dogs Today and Bradley even made the pages of Sewing
World! He featured in an article entitled 'I've Been Stitched
Up' and although he didn't make the centrefold – he did have
half a page to himself plus a HUGE photo. So far, my claim to
fame has been appearing on a calendar, in a greyhound
address book and on a mouse-mat with Ellie May . Oh – and I
did get a small picture in a local magazine called Birmingham
Life!
I am currently working on my portfolio and here are a few of
the pictures from recent photo shoots. As you can see I am
quite versatile and so far I have modelled tassels, bandanas,
beds,  'Rescue' coats and a Santa Outfit.
So just in case any of you readers are looking for a stunning
'blonde' with a curvaceous figure (29" – 19" – 29") to grace
the pages of your glossy – then look no further - this 'cover
girl' is open to offers!

LOVE FROM SAFFRON

BANDANAS

TASSELS

BEDS

SANTA OUTFIT

'RESCUE COAT'

# WHEN HARRY MET SALLY
## JERRY                SAFFY

Back in March of 2005, our ex-neighbours Tara and John Clarke rehomed a greyhound from the RGT. Like me, Jerry raced at Perry Barr track and after a few weeks settling into his new home, Tara brought him to see me. However, to use my Mum's  words, this meeting of two retired racers is unlikely to be made into a blockbuster movie to rival When Harry Met Sally.

I must admit that I tried my best to impress this tall, dark and handsome, 4 year old brindle boy, but my feminine charms were wasted on him. All right, I'm seven, but what's wrong with wanting a toy-boy? After all lots of boys find mature women very attractive. I rushed around the garden like I was back on the race track, showing off my still svelte figure, but not a flicker of interest from Jerry. So I did the circuit twice more – still not the merest sign of excitement. Well, I suppose he did manage to sway his tail but it could never be described as a joyful wag.

We were taken for a walk together but again my stunning looks didn't seem to catch his eye and even when we stood together for a photo he didn't give me a second glance. We shall meet up again from time to time no doubt, so I shall have to think up some ways to show Jerry what he's missing. If not – I am sure there are plenty more fish in the sea seeking a bouncy blonde with a gorgeous figure!!

# A BRUSH WITH EXCITEMENT!

I am sure that you have all heard about my close encounter with a RABBIT – and gosh! what a stir that caused!!. I must admit, that since moving to Rugby and teaming up with my three canine pals – there has never been a dull moment. If it's not squirrels in the back garden – it's cats.......and rabbits! out the front. At this point I would rather not be reminded that I had to eat a slice of humble pie when I didn't believe the tale about the rabbit outside the window in the days when Phoebe was here. However, they do say seeing is believing so - of course – when it made a second appearance – right before my very eyes - I had to grudgingly accept that the rabbit story was true after all!
Well, this time, the incident in question occurred one afternoon in late November. As always, our 'lookout' Roscoe doesn't miss a trick and even if he is in the dining room at the back of the house, he seems to know what is going on at the front. He launched himself into the chair by the window (the one we warn visitors not to sit on for fear of them being trampled underfoot by Roscoe) and started barking furiously . Naturally, we three joined him in a trice and followed his stare. What trespasser had the audacity to approach *our* house on this occasion........... No plucky pussy or brave bunny this time but a fearless fox! Mum rushed for her camera and house keys thinking that with the commotion we four were making – it would not be loitering for long. She squeezed out of the door - depriving us of a closer look – and took a few pictures of this urban interloper before it wandered off across the neighbours' front gardens – appearing to be in no hurry to make an exit. Well – as you can imagine we are now wondering what we can expect to visit us next  - a badger maybe or perhaps a deer? as we know they live along the railway track where we are walked each day. What a tale to tell my friends!!

# Rabbitting on………………..

You know what it's like – you've just moved to a new area and the locals can't resist telling you what happened before you arrived. Only to make you jealous over what you've missed of course and their tales are just the teeniest bit exaggerated. They delight in watching your amazement as they recount supposedly true stories of unbelievable happenings on their doorsteps. One such tale was told to me with such enthusiasm – they almost had me believing it…………….. It happened one day when the Zatonski canine family comprised Roscoe, Leah, Bradley and Phoebe. As usual, Roscoe was doing his guard dog bit – and back up, in the form of Leah and Phoebe, was ready and waiting to assist in scaring off unwanted visitors. Bradley, of course did not participate in such childish games and was no doubt taking a nap – a feat nigh on impossible given the racket the three others created. On this occasion the fervour was such that the interloper could not be human but must be feline. Phoebe, I'm told, was beside herself – staring through the window to the ground below and wailing like a banshee. However, the 'visitor', rumour has it, was none other than a lop-eared RABBIT. Well – as you can imagine – I took all this with a pinch of salt and put it down to being a bit of a fairy tale. Fantastic stories have a habit of being enlarged over time and what was probably a neighbour's small dog – soon became a cat and then a rabbit just to sensationalise the event. It's amazing what some dogs will do to impress the newcomer…..

However...........I have just had to eat a huge slice of humble pie. This morning, Roscoe alerted us dogs to a movement outside the lounge window. We all followed his intense stare and what should be there but a lop-eared RABBIT!! Mark and Judy realised this was an escaped pet but despite several attempts at catching it – the creature was far more nimble than it appeared. It hopped away – under the fence -  evading their grasp. Why they didn't enlist my help – I shall never know. Oh well – what a tale I shall have to tell our canine visitors when they pop round to see us! They do say truth is often stranger than fiction.
From (an ever-so slightly embarrassed)
SAFFRON

# SAFFY'S SOFA

I am sure that all of you who have ever owned a greyhound know that greys and sofas are inseparable! So being a greyhound who spends most of her day lounging around - here is my 'sofa story'
When I first arrived here, I spent each night sleeping in a comfy, roomy dog bed in the bedroom and after kennel life – this seemed the best thing since sliced bread. However,  after a few months, I thought I would check out to see how the land lies and I noticed that Ellie May spent each night on a sofa bed in the spare room. Every time I looked in on her she was either lounging on it or lying on her back and boy did she look comfortable. A sudden desire to make this mine overwhelmed me and I made it my mission to spend my nights on this sofa bed. However, no amount of trying to persuade young Ellie to give up her place to a more mature girl who has had to work for her living, had any effect whatsoever. Just to make sure it wasn't a case of 'the grass is greener' I checked out the sofa bed a couple of times during the day to see if was as cosy as Ellie made it look and sure enough it was! If persuasion wouldn't work then I had to devise plan B. Each night we four dogs share a sausage before we go to bed. We form a semicircle but no matter which position I took, Ellie always seemed to get her titbit first and then shot upstairs to bed. 'Mum' did put a folded duvet on the floor for me in the spare room but it didn't compare to the sofa. I must admit – a couple of times I did beat Ellie to it but my success rate was pretty disappointing.

However, because I am SO pretty and affectionate and I can twist my Mum round my little finger (or should that be toe?), she decided to buy me a sofa too. It's described as being terra-cotta – whatever that means – but my opinion of it is that it's terra-bly comfortable! However, as we are now both in the guest bedroom, I just hope Ellie-May doesn't snore and interrupt my beauty sleep! Well I think that's all from me - I must go and have a lie down and consult my 'wish-list' to see what I can persuade Mum to buy me next! Lots of love -

SAFFRON

# SEASON'S GREETINGS FROM SAFFY

Hi – I'm Saffron, I have been really lucky and I have found a lovely home in Rugby with Mark & Judy Zatonski and their four other rescue dogs. Boy! Have I fallen on my feet – or perhaps I should say 'my back' rather than my feet 'cos that's how I spend 90% of my day. The rest of the time is spent eating or going out for walks. Home life is wonderful and I just hope those other dogs waiting patiently in the kennels will be given the same opportunity as I have been. There are things I have to do of course – just to keep my folks happy you understand? But none of them is too arduous! I come when I am called and to show how versatile I am – I respond to the names "Bradley, Roscoe, Leah and Ellie-May" too. I will jump on the settee to keep my Mum company and I just love having my chin tickled. To show my appreciation, I chatter my teeth which Mum finds most amusing. I am keeping a close eye on the cats next door but they don't seem to want to come into our garden – I can't imagine why not! When we are sunbathing on the camp bed inside the patio doors, there is a brave squirrel that runs along the fence at the bottom of the garden. Quick as a flash we all run outside but the dratted creature is long gone when he hears 16 paws thundering across the grass. Now, just in case you think I can't count 'cos five dogs with four paws should be 20 – Bradley has no time for childish games and is far happier to stay lying on the sofa – why waste valuable sleeping time seems to be his motto!
Anyway, one of my other duties is modelling. My Mum takes loads of photos and she says I am so pretty that she just can't resist taking pictures of me in every conceivable pose.

Some of them aren't too flattering as I often sleep with my tongue hanging out! (I must make sure that Mum doesn't sneak one of 'those' photos into this book 'cos that's the sort of sneaky things Mums do! How they love to embarrass us) I have already appeared on a mouse mat with Ellie-May, sold in aid of the needy dogs in the care of Greyhound  Rescue West of England and I am also 'Miss July' on a 2005 calendar. Is there no end to my talents? Sorry if I sound conceited but I am so proud of my achievements  'cos I've only been treading the 'canine cat-walk' since the end of April this year. My Mum has also made a set of Christmas cards with me wearing four silly hats. She says she wants to show me off to all her friends and relatives. The big white, bobble on the end of the red hat was lovely and furry but sadly I wasn't allowed to toss it around and play with it. Here is a picture of me wearing  the said hat doing my best to behave
Well that's all for now – this photography lark is really tiring and I must get my beauty sleep. Us models have such busy and demanding lives but I'll try to find a few minutes from time to time to let you know how I am getting on. Happy Christmas everybody!

Lots of Love – Saffron XXX

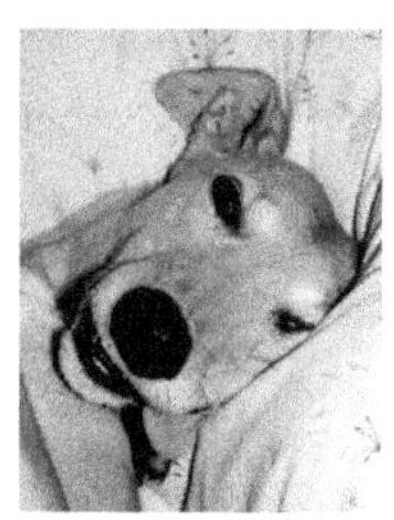

# WHEN 'PC' STANDS FOR PUSSYCAT!

When I had occasion to take Saffron to the vet recently, like many other animals waiting for their appointments, she was a quivering wreck. Being of a nervous disposition even in the least stressful of situations, she shuddered uncontrollably from head to toe (or should that be tail?), However, Saffron has asked me to stress that the damp patch on the floor was not a sign of incontinence but made by the drips from her nose! No amount of soothing words or reassuring strokes made any difference to her apprehension.

However, this all changed with the arrival of a very raucous cat in a carry cage. So loudly did this black and white 'moggy' voice it's protestations, that the noise echoed around the waiting room. Saffron was spellbound! To encounter a cat at such close quarters immediately dispelled every ounce of fear and she was totally absorbed by this opinionated feline. Her face was a picture – so much so that I wished I had my camera to capture her fascinated expression. As you no doubt know from previous 'Saffy Stories', she is not the most co-operative of photographic models and to reproduce this wonderful expression when I need her to look appealing, is nigh on impossible.

Then I had an idea!!....................

Why not put some authentic cat noises on a CD and play them when I wanted Saffron's undivided attention. That was the theory anyway! So I enlisted Mark's expertise and asked him to compile an assortment of 'miaows' on a disk so that I could play it when I wanted my 'model' to assume a photographic pose!

To gauge her reaction and to see if my cunning plan would work, Mark sat in the lounge with his laptop and searched for some authentic 'pussycat' noises. (My attempts at imitating a cat were totally ignored!)
Well............her reaction was instantaneous. What a picture of utter fascination and alertness. Saffy didn't disappoint and the effect of a vocal feline in *her* lounge was something to behold.
Without exaggeration – for the next hour – she lay on the floor staring at the PC, occasionally getting up to peer round the lid to look at the screen. Although no more 'miaows' emanated from the equipment – Saffy was totally oblivious to any other goings-on around her. It was as though she was under some hypnotic spell. By this time, even 'non -feline' noises had her hooked!
The next day when Mark set up his lap-top again - as if remembering the events of the previous evening - Saffy assumed her vigil. It seemed as though she was waiting for the PC (Pussycat) to appear from the PC when the lid was opened – as though emerging from a cat-flap. If she was upset by the absence of yesterday's 'fantasy feline' - she kept her disappointment well hidden!

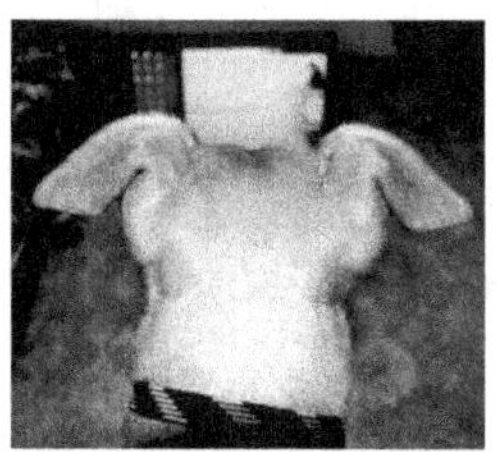

# MY BLUEBELL GIRL

As the more mature readers amongst you will no doubt remember, the Bluebell Girls used to dance at the Windmill Theatre in London - a venue which boasted 'We never close'. It would seem that although my 'Bluebell Girl' is far too young to recall this saying, she has however adopted a similar maxim - Saffron's watchword appears to be 'I never pose'.

I used to think that my dear departed Phoebe was uncooperative when it came to taking photographs but compared to Saffron she was a veritable saint! Even to get Saffy into position is a feat in itself. No amount of coaxing or cajoling will encourage her to adopt the desired stance and to get her to look even remotely interested is nigh on impossible. So in the end it comes down to pushing and pulling her into the required location. The next stage in the proceedings is to attract her attention but imitations of dog barks or whines or simulated meows, don't even raise an eyebrow, nor does the rustling of a bag of treats command even a flicker of interest. We have resorted to throwing twigs and stones in the hope that the noise will attract Saffron and make her look in the direction of the missile. It's a good job that Mark was an excellent fielder in his cricketing days or I could be in danger of being felled by one of these projectiles. I have in the past attempted to photograph Saffy whilst on my own but I have since accepted that this idea was just a figment of my imagination! Trying to stand on one end of her lead whilst tossing a twig backwards over my head and operate the camera at the same time makes juggling three balls in the air look like child's play! So the assistance of a third party is essential. All I can say is thank goodness for digital cameras! No longer must I wait a few days to view 36 disappointing photographs – I can now see my futile attempts instantly!

Stunning as Saffron is, it is amazing how bored and uninterested she can look. I am of the opinion that greyhounds generally don't seem to find that modelling is one of their vocations in life unless of course they are snapped whilst dozing on their backs with their legs in the air!
I feel that when I do get a pleasing shot of my pretty blonde girl, I should be congratulated more for my patience and perseverance than my photographic skills. Each picture should be accompanied by a blow by blow account of the number of pictures I needed to take, the length of time I spent crouching in the undergrowth amongst brambles and nettles and the amount of encouragement and persuasion (and bribery)  my assistant required, to allow me to get a picture of my stunning 'Bluebell Girl!'

# A ROLL IN ADVERTISING?

Should  you ever come to stay with us – let me give you a piece of good advice. Never, ever leave the bathroom door ajar – however short you may be caught!
The reason for this recommendation is not so much a matter of privacy but more one of convenience or perhaps I should say 'inconvenience'.  Saffron has decided to assume the role of the Andrex puppy! She may not be a Labrador – nor a puppy for that matter but one flick of her tail and she can whisk away the toilet roll in seconds. The sheets are deftly unravelled and as Saffy leaves the room – so does the roll. The long ribbon of tissue follows in her wake and it requires a very swift reaction to catch the last few sheets as they disappear from view. She seems totally oblivious to the consequences of her actions…. leaving one 'high' but far from the proverbial 'dry'!

Maybe she is rehearsing for the role of understudy, should the opportunity arise for her acting skills to be required? However, I would much prefer a 'normal' 'boring' couch potato with much lesser aspirations than a budding star of stage and screen. For apart from the obvious inconvenience - rewinding  the sheets is such a laborious task!

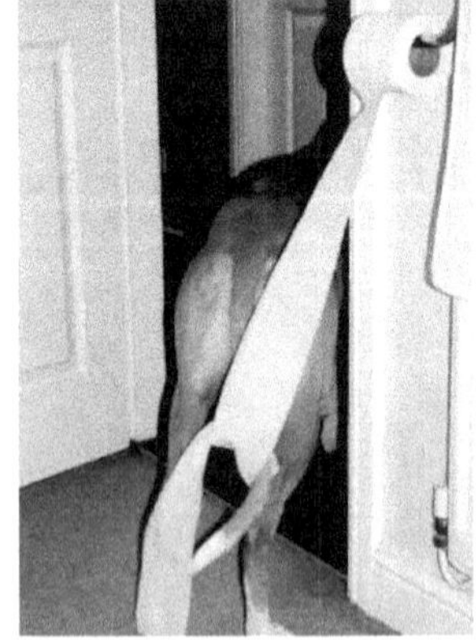

# FAREWELL MY LOVELY
## SAFFRON – aka Jamstyle Joy
### 23/8/1997 – 12/4/2006

When I had to say goodbye to you on 12 April this year my world truly fell apart. You were found to have bone cancer in your shoulder and it was so aggressive that I could see the lump grow bigger daily during the last fortnight. Although it did make you limp, it only seemed to cause you pain when you leapt onto the settee or had to go up or down steps and for this reason, I slept downstairs with you for your final two weeks. Up until the morning of 12 April you were generally still your happy and enthusiastic self. From day one in April 2004 your were the 'perfect' girl – beautiful, loving and laid back although you did have your moments when you would play wildly with a toy for a short while. Almost from the start you were relaxed in our company but should a visitor arrive you would run away and hide or should a stranger approach whilst you were out for a walk, then you would cower behind me, quivering with a worried expression. Children were even more of a trauma, on hearing a single scream you would turn tail and do your best to get as far away as possible. You didn't have to see a child but just hear them shouting and you would become a shy and nervous girl. Even when they approached you very slowly and cautiously, uttering words of comfort and desperately wanting to stroke your beautiful coat, you found your fear difficult to overcome. But I didn't mind one bit – you trusted us and that was all that mattered to me. You loved to lie with me on the sofa, your head on my shoulder, sometimes chattering your teeth with pleasure and at other times whining when I stopped stroking you. Letting you go broke my heart but I couldn't bear to see you in pain. I shall treasure the poems, stories and photos of you and although the pain gets easier it never goes away.

Thank you for bringing such joy to my life
Farewell my lovely Saffron.

Copyright © 2023 Judy Zatonski

ISBN: 9781916981003

9 781916 981003